Anonymous

The Letters of the Celebrated Junius

A more complete edition than any yet published - Volume I

Anonymous

The Letters of the Celebrated Junius
A more complete edition than any yet published - Volume I

ISBN/EAN: 9783337017378

Printed in Europe, USA, Canada, Australia, Japan

Cover: Foto ©ninafisch / pixelio.de

More available books at **www.hansebooks.com**

LETTERS

OF THE CELEBRATED

JUNIUS.

A MORE COMPLETE EDITION
THAN ANY YET PUBLISHED.

IN TWO VOLUMES.

VOLUME I.

LONDON:
PRINTED IN THE YEAR M,DCC,LXXXIII.

ADVERTISEMENT.

THIS edition of the celebrated Letters of Junius, is given as a more complete one than any yet published. In what is called the author's own edition, THREE FOURTHS of the Letter respecting the Bill of Rights, the most important one in the collection, were omitted. All these omissions are restored to their proper places in this edition.

FOURTEEN LETTERS are also added to this edition: They are either Letters written by Junius, or Letters to which he has replied; and, on that account, justice seemed to require, that they should be ranged along with his answers to them. These Letters are marked with a star. A variety of Explanatory Notes have also been added; some of which have been noticed in the contents; but the whole of them were too numerous to be so distinguished.

IT is proper to observe, that the Letters signed Philo Junius were written by
Junius,

ADVERTISEMENT.

Junius. In this edition, a miftake committed in the author's edition has been avoided. In that edition, the Letter of Philo Junius, dated May 22d, 1771, is inferted twice; the firft time in Volume Firft as a *Note* to the twentieth Letter, and the fecond time in Volume Second, as the forty-fixth Letter.

M. DE

LIBERTY OF THE PRESS.

"WHOEVER considers what it is,
" that constitutes the moving princi-
" ple of what we call great affairs, and the
" invincible sensibility of man to the opinion
" of his fellow-creatures, will not hesitate to
" affirm that, if it were possible for the li-
" berty of the press to exist in a despotic go-
" vernment, and, (what is not less difficult)
" for it to exist without changing the consti-
" tution, this liberty of the press would a-
" lone form a counterpoise to the power of
" the prince. If, for example, in an empire
" of the East, a sanctuary could be found,
" which, rendered respectable by the ancient
" religion of the people, might insure safety
" to those, who should bring thither their
" observations of any kind; and that, from
" thence, printed papers should issue, which
" under a certain seal, might be equally re-
" spected; and which, in their daily appear-
" ance, should examine and freely discuss the
" conduct of the Cadis, the Bashaws, the
" Vizir, the Divan, and the Sultan himself,
" that would introduce immediately some

ERRATUM: Letter XXXIII. should be numbered XXXII. and Letter XXXIV. should be XXXIII. and so on to the end.

OF VOLUME FIRST.

LETTER I.

POLITICAL character of Englishmen: alarming state of the nation: plan of government since his present Majesty's accession: characters of the present and former Ministers: America: summary view of our condition.
Notes: Character of the Duke of Grafton; his conduct to the Marquis of Rockingham. Junius and Lord Mansfield's opinion of Mr. Pitt's and Lord Camden's declamations in favour of America.
page 1—18

LETTER II.

Sir William Draper's defence of the Marquis of Granby.
Notes: Sir William Draper's embroidered nightgown; his healing letter from Clifton 19—26

LETTER III.

Junius's reply to Sir William Draper; reviews again Lord Granby's character; and calls Sir William to the defence of his own 27—34

LETTER IV.

Sir William Draper's defence of Lord Granby and himself 35—43

LETTER V.

Junius in mercy to Lord Granby confines his questions to Sir William's conduct. 43—46

LETTER VI.

Sir William's answers, and questions in retort 46—48

LET-

LETTER VII.

Junius to Sir William Draper; the nature of the rewards beſtowed on the latter; Junius's advice to him.

Note: Sir William drops the conteſt at Lord Granby's requeſt   48—52

LETTER VIII.

Junius to the Duke of Grafton, on the pardon of M'Quirk

Note: The Royal Warrant for the pardon of M'Quirk   52—59

*LETTER IX.

A vindication of the Duke of Grafton by a Volunteer   59—66

LETTER X.

Junius to the Duke of Grafton on the fatality that attends the Duke and his friends; in anſwer to the Volunteer   66—71

*LETTER XI.

The Volunteer's anſwer   71—73

LETTER XII.

Junius to Mr. Edward Weſton.

Note: Mr. Weſton's appointments: a charge againſt him denied   73—75

*LETTER XIII.

The Tears of Sedition, a monody on Junius, by Poeticaſtos.   75—77

*LETTER XIV.

Junius to Poeticaſtos   77

*LETTERS XV. AND XVI.

Poeticaſtos to Junius   78—81

LET.

CONTENTS.

*LETTER XVII.
Hector to Poeticastos   81—82

*LETTER XVIII.
Poeticastos's resolve in regard to Junius   82

LETTER XIX.
Junius to the Duke of Grafton; reviews his Grace's conduct as a public and private man; Mr. Wilkes, Mr. Luttrell, and Miss Parsons
    Note: A letter from a Duke to Ann Parsons, with her answer   83—92

LETTER XX.
Junius considers his Grace's character and conduct merely as a subject of curious speculation.
    Notes relating to his Grace   92—104

LETTER XXI.
Philo Junius states the facts advanced by Junius, and asserts their truth   104—107

*LETTER XXII.
Old Noll's reply to the charges against the Duke of Grafton   107—111

LETTER XXIII.
Philo Junius to Old Noll   111—117

LETTER XXIV.
Junius to the Duke of Grafton. The system of government laid open   117—126

LETTER XXV.
Junius states the question relating to the Middlesex election   126—133

LETTER XXVI.
Philo Junius vindicates the opinions of Junius on the Middlesex election   133—138

LET-

LETTER XXVII.

Junius to Sir William Blackstone, in answer to his pamphlet on the Middlesex election   138—146

LETTER XXVIII.

Philo Junius in vindication of Junius's strictures on Sir William Blackstone, and quotes an ingenious sarcasm of Sir Fletcher Norton's   146—148

LETTER XXIX.

Sir William Blackstone's answer to Junius   148—158

LETTER XXX.

Junius's reply   158—167

LETTER XXXI.

Philo Junius on Mr. Walpole's case   167—171

LETTER XXXIII.

Junius in explanation of his last letter.   171—173

LETTER XXXIV.

Argument against fact, or a new system of political logic by Ministry; with a conclusion by Philo Junius
173—178

*LETTER XXXV.

Junius to Junia, a very curious double entendre
178—180

LETTER XXXVI.

Junius to the Duke of Bedford. His Grace's character and conduct, and those of his friends.
  Notes: *Marquis of Tavistock; Lord Bute and his Grace; a Borough; Corporation of Bedford; Mr. Humphreys, Mr. Rigby, Lord Chesterfield, his Grace; Lord Egremont; Mr. Grenville; Lord Weymouth; the Bedford Party; his Grace's death*   180—195

LET-

LETTER XXXVII.
Sir William Draper renews the conteſt with Junius on his own account, and calls on him to produce himſelf   195—198

LETTER XXXVIII.
Junius to Sir William Draper. Sir William has no right to his name, having begun the attack on Junius, he has no right to know him by any other name   198—202

LETTER XXXIX.
Sir William Draper's word at parting, and vindication of the Duke of Bedford.
  Notes: Junius ſuppoſed to ſend Sir William on his travels   203—209

LETTER XL.
Junius to Sir William Draper. The latter the bittereſt enemy to his own friends   209—216

*LETTER XLI.
Frances to Junius, in vindication of the Duke of Bedford. An inſtance of his Grace's humanity 216—218

LETTER XLII.
Junius to Frances, applauds her gratitude, but her letter proves nothing in the preſent argument 218—219

LETTER XLIII.
Philo Junius in reply to Modeſtus's defence of Sir William Draper and the Duke of Bedford   218—226

LETTER XLIV.
Junius on the reſcue of General Ganſell.
  Note: General Ganſell's caſe; brigade orders; his trial and death   226—237

LET-

LETTER XLV.
Philo Junius defends Junius's letter on General Ganfell's affair
237—243

*LETTER XLVI.
Modeſtus accepts a challenge given by Junius on Gen. Ganſell's reſcue, and replies to his letter 243—249

*LETTER XLVII.
Modeſtus reminds Junius of the challenge 249—254

LETTER XLVIII.
Junius's anſwer to Modeſtus 254—256

LETTER XLIX.
Junius to the Duke of Grafton on Meſſrs. Hine, Burgoyne, and Vaughan
   Note: Col. Burgoyne's conduct and fine 256—258

LETTER L.
Junius to the Duke of Grafton. Farther particulars relating to Hine, Burgoyne, and Vaughan.
   Note: Vaughan's trial, and Lord Mansfield's ſpeech 258—263

LETTERS

OF

JUNIUS, &c.

LETTER I.

TO THE PRINTER OF THE PUBLIC ADVERTISER.

SIR,   21 *January* 1769.

THE submission of a free people to the executive authority of government is no more than a compliance with laws, which they themselves have enacted. While the national honour is firmly maintained abroad, and while justice is impartially administered at home, the obedience of the subject will be voluntary, chearful, and I might almost say unlimited. A generous nation is grateful even for the preservation of its rights, and willingly extends the respect due to the office of a good prince into an affection for his person. Loyalty, in the heart and understanding of an Englishman, is a rational attachment to the guardian of the laws. Prejudices and passion have sometimes carried it to a criminal length; and, whatever foreigners may imagine, we know that Englishmen have erred as much in a miftaken zeal for particular perfons and families, as they ever did in defence of what they thought moft dear and interefting to themfelves.

It naturally fills us with refentment, to fee fuch a temper infulted and abufed. In reading the hiftory of a free people, whofe rights have been invaded, we are interefted in their caufe. Our own feelings tell us how long they ought to have fubmitted, and at what moment it would have been treachery to themfelves not to have refifted. How much warmer will be our refentment, if experience fhould bring the fatal example home to ourfelves!

The fituation of this country is alarming enough to roufe the attention of every man, who pretends to a concern for the public welfare. Appearances juftify fufpicion; and, when the fafety of a nation is at ftake, fufpicion is a juft ground of enquiry. Let us enter into it with candour and decency. Refpect is due to the ftation of minifters; and, if a refolution muft at laft be taken, there is none fo likely to be fupported with firmnefs, as that which has been adopted with moderation.

The ruin or profperity of a ftate depends
fo

so much upon the administration of its government, that, to be acquainted with the merit of a ministry, we need only observe the condition of the people. If we see them obedient to the laws, prosperous in their industry, united at home, and respected abroad, we may reasonably presume that their affairs are conducted by men of experience, abilities, and virtue. If, on the contrary, we see an universal spirit of distrust and dissatisfaction, a rapid decay of trade, dissentions in all parts of the empire, and a total loss of respect in the eyes of foreign powers, we may pronounce, without hesitation, that the government of that country is weak, distracted, and corrupt. The multitude, in all countries, are patient to a certain point. Ill usage may rouse their indignation, and hurry them into excesses, but the original fault is in government. Perhaps there never was an instance of a change in the circumstances and temper of a whole nation, so sudden and extraordinary as that which the misconduct of ministers has, within these few years, produced in Great Britain. When our gracious sovereign ascended the throne, we were a flourishing and a contented people. If the personal virtues of a king could have insured the happiness of his subjects, the scene could not have altered so entirely as it has done. The idea of uniting all parties, of trying all characters, and distributing the offices of state by rotation, was gracious and benevolent to an extreme, though it has not yet produced the many salutary effects which were intended by it. To say nothing of the wisdom of such a plan, it undoubtedly arose from an unbounded goodness of heart, in which folly had no share. It was not a capricious partiality to new faces;—it was not a natural turn for low intrigue; nor was it the treacherous amusement of double and triple negotiations. No, Sir, it arose from a continued anxiety, in the purest of all possible hearts, for the general welfare. Unfortunately for us, the event has not been answerable to the design. After a rapid succession of changes we are reduced to that state, which hardly any change can mend. Yet there is no extremity of distress, which of itself ought to reduce a great nation to despair. It is not the disorder but the physician;—it is not a casual concurrence of calamitous circumstances, it is the pernicious hand of government,* which alone can make a whole people desperate.

WITHOUT much political sagacity, or any extraordinary depth of observation, we need only mark how the principal departments of the state are bestowed, and look no farther

farther for the true cause of every mischief that befals us.

* THE finances of a nation, sinking under its debts and expences, are committed to a

young

* When the Duke of Grafton first entered into office, it was the fashion of the times to suppose that young men might have wisdom without experience. They thought so themselves, and the most important affairs of this country were committed to the first trial of their abilities. His Grace had honourably flesht his maiden sword in the field of opposition, and had gone through all the discipline of the minority with credit. He dined at Wildman's, railed at favourites, looked up to Lord Chatham with astonishment, and was the declared advocate of Mr. Wilkes. It afterwards pleased his Grace to enter into administration with his friend Lord Rockingham, and, in a very little time, it pleased his Grace to abandon him. He then accepted of the treasury upon terms which Lord Temple had disdained. For a short time his submission to Lord Chatham was unlimited. He could not answer a private letter without Lord Chatham's permission. I presume he was then learning his trade, for he soon set up for himself. Until he declared himself the minister, his character had been but little understood. From that moment a system of conduct, directed by passion and caprice, not only reminds us that he is a young man, but a young man without solidity or judgment. One day he desponds and threatens to resign. The next, he finds his blood heated, and swears to his friend he is determined to go on. In his public measures we have seen no proof either of ability or consistence. The Stamp-act had been

repealed

young nobleman already ruined by play. Introduced to act under the auspices of Lord Chatham, and left at the head of affairs by that nobleman's retreat, he became minister by

repealed (no matter how unwisely) under the preceding administration. The colonies had reason to triumph, and were returning to their good humour. The point was decided, when this young man thought proper to revive it. Without either plan or necessity, he adopts the spirit of Mr. Grenville's measures, and renews the question of taxation in a form more odious and less effectual than that of the law, which had been repealed.

WITH respect to the invasion of Corsica, it will be matter of parliamentary enquiry, whether he has carried on a secret negociation with the French court, in terms contradictory to the resolution of council, and to the instructions drawn up thereupon by his Majesty's secretary of state. If it shall appear that he has quitted the line of his department to betray the honour and security of his country, and if there be a power sufficient to protect him, in such a case, against public justice, the constitution of Great Britain is at an end.

HIS standing foremost in the persecution of Mr. Wilkes, if former declarations and connections be considered, is base and contemptible. The man, whom he now brands with treason and blasphemy, but a very few years ago was the Duke of Grafton's friend, nor is his identity altered, except by his misfortunes.—In the last instance of his Grace's judgment and inconsistency, we see him, after trying and deserting every party, throw himself into the arms of a set of men, whose political principles he had always pretended to abhor.

These

by accident; but deserting the principles and professions, which gave him a moment's popularity, we see him, from every honourable engagement to the public, an apostate by design.

These men I doubt not will teach him the folly of his conduct better than I can. They grasp at every thing, and will soon push him from his seat. His private history would but little deserve our attention, if he had not voluntarily brought it into public notice. I will not call the amusements of a young man criminal, though I think they become his age better than his station. There is a period, at which the most unruly passions are gratified or exhausted, and which leaves the mind clear and undisturbed in its attention to business. His Grace's gallantry would be offended, if we were to suppose him within many years of being thus qualified for public affairs. As for the rest, making every allowance for the frailty of human nature, I can make none for a continued breach of public decorum; nor can I believe that man very zealous for the interest of his country, who sets her opinion at defiance. This nobleman, however, has one claim to respect, since it has pleased our gracious Sovereign to make him prime Minister of Great Britain.

July 10, 1765. The Duke of Grafton took the office of Secretary of State, with an engagement to support the administration of the Marquis of Rockingham, just then formed.

May 23, 1766. He resigned under pretence that he could not act without Mr. Pitt, nor bear to see Mr. Wilkes abandoned; but that under Mr. Pitt he would
act

sign. As for business, the world yet knows nothing of his talents or resolution; unless a wayward, wavering inconsistency be a mark of genius, and caprice a demonstration of spirit. It may be said, perhaps, that it is his Grace's province, as surely it is his passion, rather to distribute than to save the public money; and that while Lord North is Chancellor of the Exchequer, the First Lord of the Treasury may be as thoughtless and extravagant as he pleases. I hope however he will not rely too much on the fertility of Lord North's genius for finance. His Lordship is yet to give us the first proof of his abilities: It may be candid to suppose that he has hitherto voluntarily concealed his talents; intending perhaps to astonish the world, when we least expect it, with a knowledge of trade, a choice of expedients, and a depth of resources, equal to the necessities, and far beyond the hopes of his country. He must now exert the whole power of his capacity, if he would wish us to forget,

that

act in any office. This was the signal of Lord Rockingham's dismission. When Lord Chatham came in, the Duke got possession of the Treasury.

July 30, 1766. Mr. Pitt was created Earl of Chatham, and appointed Lord Privy Seal.

August 2, 1766. The Duke of Grafton was appointed First Lord of the Treasury, in room of the Marquis of Rockingham.

that since he has been in office, no plan has been formed, no syftem adhered to, nor any one important meafure adopted for the relief of public credit. If his plan for the fervice of the current year be not irrevocably fixed on, let me warn him to think ferioufly of confequences before he ventures to increafe the public debt. Outraged and oppreffed as we are, this nation will not bear, after a fix years peace, to fee new millions borrowed, without an eventual diminution of debt, or reduction of intereft. The attempt might roufe a fpirit of refentment, which might reach beyond the facrifice of a minifter. As to the debt upon the civil lift, the people of England expect that it will not be paid without a ftrict enquiry how it was incurred. If it muft be paid by parliament, let me advife the Chancellor of the Exchequer to think of fome better expedient than a lottery. To fupport an expenfive war, or in circumftances of abfolute neceffity, a lottery may perhaps be allowable; but, befides that it is at all times the very worft way of raifing money upon the people, I think it ill becomes the Royal dignity to have the debts of a King provided for, like the repairs of a country bridge, or a decayed hofpital. The management of the King's affairs in the Houfe of Commons cannot be more difgraced than it has been. * A

* Lord North.

lead-

leading Minister repeatedly called down for absolute ignorance;—ridiculous motions ridiculously withdrawn;—deliberate plans disconcerted, and a week's preparation of graceful oratory lost in a moment, give us some, though not an adequate idea of Lord North's parliamentary abilities and influence. Yet before he had the misfortune of being Chancellor of the Exchequer, he was neither an object of derision to his enemies, nor of melancholy pity to his friends.

A SERIES of inconsistent measures has alienated the colonies from their duty as subjects, and from their natural affection to their common country. When Mr. Grenville was placed at the head of the Treasury, he felt the impossibility of Great Britain's supporting such an establishment as her former successes had made indispensable, and at the same time of giving any sensible relief to foreign trade, and to the weight of the public debt. He thought it equitable that those parts of the empire, which had benefited most by the expences of the war, should contribute something to the expences of the peace; and he had no doubt of the constitutional right vested in parliament to raise the contribution. But, unfortunately for this country, Mr. Grenville was at any rate to be distressed because he was Minister, and Mr. Pitt and Lord Camden

were

were to be the patrons of America, because they were in opposition. Their declamation gave spirit and argument to the colonies, and while perhaps they meant no more than a ruin of a minister, they in effect divided one half of the empire from the other*.

UNDER one administration the stamp act is made†; under the second it is repealed‡; under the third, in spite of all experience, a new mode of taxing the colonies is invented§, and a question revived, which ought to have been buried in oblivion. In these circumstances a new office is established for the business of the plantations, and the Earl of Hillsborough called forth, at a most critical

---

* THIS, though said upwards of *six years* before the war, has turned out too true a prophecy. It is worthy of remark that two great characters, who were very far from being attached to each other, yet thought nearly alike on the American business. Lord Mansfield, two years before the above letter was written, in a speech against the suspending and dispensing prerogative, reminded the House of what had been told them the year before, " *that they would import rebellion from America.*"

† GRENVILLE Administration.

‡ ROCKINGHAM Administration.

§ The tea duty laid by the Chatham and Grafton Administration.

season.

feafon, to govern America. The choice at leaft announced to us a man of fuperior capacity and knowledge. Whether he be fo or not, let his difpatches as far as they have appeared, let his meafures as far as they have operated, determine for him. In the former we have feen ftrong affertions without proof, declamation without argument, and violent cenfures without dignity or moderation; but neither correctnefs in the compofition, nor judgment in the defign. As for his meafures, let it be remembered, that he was called upon to conciliate and unite; and that, when he entered into office, the moft refractory of the colonies were ftill difpofed to proceed by the conftitutional methods of petition and remonftrance. Since that period they have been driven into exceffes little fhort of rebellion. Petitions have been hindered from reaching the throne; and the continuance of one of the principal affemblies refted upon an arbitrary condition§, which, confidering the temper they were in, it was impoffible they fhould comply with, and which would have availed nothing as to the general queftion, if it had been complied with. So violent, and I believe I may call it fo unconftitutional an exertion of the prerogative, to fay nothing of

§ That they fhould retract one of their refolutions, and erafe the entry of it.

the

the weak, injudicious terms in which it was conveyed, gives us as humble an opinion of his lordſhip's capacity, as it does of his temper and moderation. While we are at peace with other nations, our military force may perhaps be ſpared to ſupport the Earl of Hillſborough's meaſures in America. Whenever that force ſhall be neceſſarily withdrawn or diminiſhed, the difmiſſion of ſuch a miniſter will neither conſole us for his imprudence, nor remove the ſettled reſentment of a people, who, complaining of an act of the legiſlature, are outraged by an unwarrantable ſtretch of prerogative, and, ſupporting their claims by argument, are inſulted with declamation.

DRAWING lots would be a prudent and reaſonable method of appointing the officers of ſtate, compared to a late diſpoſition of the ſecretary's office. Lord Rochford was acquainted with the affairs and temper of the ſouthern courts: Lord Weymouth was equally qualified for either department*. By what unaccountable caprice has it happened, that the latter, who pretends to no experience what-

* It was ſaid, that this remove was made out of compliment to the Duke of Choiſeuil, the French Miniſter, as Lord Rochford, when Ambaſſador in France, had offended his Grace by ſome ſpirited repreſentations.

ſoever

soever, is removed to the most important of the two departments, and the former by preference placed in an office, where his experience can be of no use to him? Lord Weymouth had distinguished himself in his first employment by a spirited if not judicious conduct. He had animated the civil magistrate beyond the tone of civil authority, and had directed the operations of the army to more than military execution. Recovered from the errors of his youth, from the distraction of play, and the bewitching smiles of Burgundy, behold him exerting the whole strength of his clear, unclouded faculties, in the service of the crown. It was not the heat of midnight excesses, nor ignorance of the laws, nor furious spirit of the house of Bedford; No, Sir, when this respectable minister interposed his authority between the magistrate, and the people, and signed the mandate, on which, for aught he knew, the lives of thousands depended, he did it from the deliberate motion of his heart, supported by the best of his judgment.

It has lately been a fashion to pay a compliment to the bravery and generosity of the commander in chief[*], at the expence of his understanding. They who love him least make no question of his courage, while his

[*] The late Marquis of Granby.

friends

friends dwell chiefly on the facility of his
difpofition. Admitting him to be as brave
as a total abfence of all feeling and reflection
can make him, let us fee what fort of merit he
derives from the remainder of his character.
If it be generofity to accumulate in his own
perfon and family a number of lucrative em-
ployments; to provide, at the public expence, for every creature that bears the name
of Manners; and, neglecting the merit and
fervices of the reft of the army, to heap pro-
motions upon his favourites and dependants,
the prefent commander in chief is the moft
generous man alive. Nature has been fpa-
ring of her gifts to this noble lord; but
where birth and fortune are united, we expect
the noble pride and independence of a man
of fpirit, not the fervile, humiliating com-
plaifance of a courtier. As to the goodnefs
of his heart, if a proof of it be taken from
the facility of never refufing, what conclufion fhall we draw from the indecency of
never performing? And if the difcipline of
the army be in any degree preferved, what
thanks are due to a man, whofe cares, noto-
rioufly confined to filling up vacancies, have
degraded the office of commander in chief
into a broker of commiffions*!

* Thefe animadverfions brought forward Sir William Draper, who though poffeffed of great literary talents, could not cope with Junius.

WITH

With respect to the navy, I shall only say, that this country is so highly indebted to Sir Edward Hawke, that no expence should be spared to secure to him an honourable and affluent retreat.

The pure and impartial administration of justice is perhaps the firmest bond to secure a chearful submission of the people, and to engage their affections to government. It is not sufficient that questions of private right or wrong are justly decided, nor that judges are superior to the vileness of pecuniary corruption. Jefferies himself, when the court had no interest, was an upright judge. A court of justice may be subject to another sort of bias, more important and pernicious, as it reaches beyond the interest of individuals, and affects the whole community. A judge under the influence of government, may be honest enough in the decision of private causes, yet a traitor to the public. When a victim is marked out by the ministry, this judge will offer himself to perform the sacrifice. He will not scruple to prostitute his dignity, and betray the sanctity of his office, whenever an arbitrary point is to be carried for government, or the resentment of a court to be gratified.

THESE

These principles and proceedings, odious and contemptible as they are, in effect are no less injudicious. A wise and generous people are roused by every appearance of oppressive, unconstitutional measures, whether those measures are supported only by the power of government, or masked under the forms of a court of justice. Prudence and self-preservation will oblige the most moderate dispositions to make it a common cause, even with a man whose conduct they censure, if they see him persecuted in a way, which the real spirit of the laws will not justify. The facts, on which these remarks are founded, are too notorious to require an application.

This, Sir, is the detail. In one view behold a nation overwhelmed with debt; her revenues wasted; her trade declining; the affections of her colonies alienated; the duty of the magistrate transferred to the soldiery; a gallant army, which never fought unwillingly but against their fellow subjects, mouldering away for want of the direction of a man of common abilities and spirit; and, in the last instance, the administration of justice become odious and suspected to the whole body of the people. This deplorable scene admits of but one addition---that we are governed by counsels, from which a reasonable

sonable man can expect no remedy but poison, no relief but death.

If, by the immediate interposition of Providence, it were possible for us to escape a crisis so full of terror and despair, posterity will not believe the history of the present times. They will either conclude that our distresses were imaginary, or that we had the good fortune to be governed by men of acknowledged integrity and wisdom: they will not believe it possible that their ancestors could have survived, or recovered from so desperate a condition, while a Duke of Grafton was Prime Minister, a Lord North Chancellor of the Exchequer, a Weymouth and a Hillsborough Secretaries of State, a Granby Commander in Chief, and a Mansfield chief criminal Judge of the kingdom.

JUNIUS.

LETTER

LETTER II.

TO THE PRINTER OF THE PUBLIC ADVERTISER.

SIR, 26 *January*, 1769.

THE kingdom swarms with such numbers of felonious robbers of private character and virtue, that no honest or good man is safe; especially as these cowardly base assassins stab in the dark, without having the courage to sign their real names to their malevolent and wicked productions. A writer, who signs himself Junius, in the Public Advertiser of the 21st instant, opens the deplorable situation of his country in a very affecting manner; with a pompous parade of his candour and decency, he tells us, that we see dissentions in all parts of the empire, an universal spirit of distrust and dissatisfaction, and a total loss of respect towards us in the eyes of foreign powers. But this writer, with all his boasted candour, has not told us the real cause of the evils he so pathetically enumerates. I shall take the liberty to explain the cause for him. Junius, and such writers as himself, occasion all the mischief complained of, by falsely and maliciously

ously

ously traducing the beſt characters in the kingdom. For when our deluded people at home, and foreigners abroad, read the poiſonous and inflammatory libels that are daily publiſhed with impunity, to vilify thoſe who are any way diſtinguiſhed by their good qualities and eminent virtues: when they find no notice taken of, or reply given to theſe ſlanderous tongues and pens, their concluſion is, that both the miniſters and the nation have been fairly deſcribed; and they act accordingly. I think it therefore the duty of every good citizen to ſtand forth, and endeavour to undeceive the public, when the vileſt arts are made uſe of to defame and blacken the brighteſt characters among us. An eminent author affirms it to be almoſt as criminal to hear a worthy man traduced, without attempting his juſtification, as to be the author of the calumny againſt him. For my own part, I think it a ſort of miſpriſion of treaſon againſt ſociety. No man therefore who knows Lord Granby, can poſſibly hear ſo good and great a character moſt vilely abuſed, without a warm and juſt indignation againſt this Junius, this high-prieſt of envy, malice, and all uncharitableneſs, who has endeavoured to ſacrifice our beloved commander in chief at the altars of his horrid deities. Nor is the injury done to his lordſhip alone, but to the whole nation, which may

too

too soon feel the contempt, and consequently the attacks of our late enemies, if they can be induced to believe that the person, on whom the safety of these kingdoms so much depends, is unequal to his high station, and destitute of those qualities which form a good general. One would have thought that his lordship's services in the cause of his country, from the battle of Culloden to his most glorious conclusion of the late war, might have entitled him to common respect and decency at least; but this uncandid indecent writer has gone so far as to turn one of the most amiable men of the age into a stupid, unfeeling, and senseless being; possessed indeed of a personal courage, but void of those essential qualities which distinguish the commander from the common soldier.

A VERY long, uninterrupted, impartial, I will add, a most disinterested friendship with Lord Granby, gives me the right to affirm, that all Junius's assertions are false and scandalous. Lord Granby's courage, though of the brightest and most ardent kind, is among the lowest of his numerous good qualities; he was formed to excel in war by nature's liberality to his mind as well as person. Educated and instructed by his most noble father, and a most spirited as well as excellent scholar, the present Bishop of Bangor,

gor, he was trained to the nicest sense of honour, and to the truest and noblest sort of pride, that of never doing or suffering a mean action. A sincere love and attachment to his king and country, and to their glory, first impelled him to the field, where he never gained aught but honour. He impaired, through his bounty, his own fortune; for his bounty, which this writer would in vain depreciate, is founded upon the noblest of the human affections, it flows from a heart melting to goodness from the most refined humanity. Can a man, who is described as unfeeling, and void of reflection, be constantly employed in seeking proper objects on whom to exercise those glorious virtues of compassion and generosity? The distressed officer, the soldier, the widow, the orphan, and a long list besides, know that vanity has no share in his frequent donations: he gives, because he feels their distresses. Nor has he ever been rapacious with one hand to be bountiful with the other; yet this uncandid Junius would insinuate, that the dignity of the commander in chief is depraved into the base office of a commission broker; that is, Lord Granby bargains for the sale of commissions; for it must have this meaning, if it has any at all. But where is the man living who can justly charge his lordship with such mean practices? Why does not Junius

produce

produce him? Junius knows that he has no other means of wounding this hero, than from some missile weapon, shot from an obscure corner: He seeks, as all such defamatory writers do,

> *spargere voces*
> *In Vulgum ambiguas,*

to raise suspicion in the minds of the people. But I hope that my countrymen will be no longer imposed upon by artful and designing men, or by wretches, who, bankrupts in business, in fame, and in fortune, mean nothing more than to involve this country in the same common ruin with themselves. Hence it is, that they are constantly aiming their dark and too often fatal weapons against those who stand forth as the bulwark of our national safety. Lord Granby was too conspicuous a mark not to be their object. He is next attacked for being unfaithful to his promises and engagements: Where are Junius's proofs? Although I could give some instances, where a breach of promise would be a virtue, especially in the case of those who would pervert the open, unsuspecting moments of convivial mirth, into sly, insidious applications for preferment, or party systems, and would endeavour to surprise a good man, who cannot bear to see any one leave him
dissatisfied,

diſſatisfied, into unguarded promiſes. Lord Granby's attention to his own family and relations is called ſelfiſh. Had he not attended to them, when fair and juſt opportunities preſented themſelves, I ſhould have thought him unfeeling, and void of reflection indeed. How are any man's friends or relations to be provided for, but from the influence and protection of the patron? It is unfair to ſuppoſe that Lord Granby's friends have not as much merit as the friends of any other great man: If he is generous at the public expence, as Junius invidiouſly calls it, the public is at no more expence for his lordſhip's friends, than it would be if any other ſet of men poſſeſſed thoſe offices. The charge is ridiculous!

The laſt charge againſt Lord Granby is of a moſt ſerious and alarming nature indeed. Junius aſſerts, that the army is mouldering away for want of the direction of a man of common abilities and ſpirit, The preſent condition of the army gives the directeſt lie to his aſſertions. It was never upon a more reſpectable footing with regard to diſcipline, and all the eſſentials that can form good ſoldiers. Lord Ligonier delivered a firm and noble palladium of our ſafeties into Lord Granby's hands, who has kept it in the ſame good order in which he received it. The

ſtricteſt

strictest care has been taken to fill up the vacant commissions, with such gentlemen as have the glory of their ancestors to support, as well as their own, and are doubly bound to the cause of their king and country, from motives of private property, as well as public spirit. The adjutant-general, who has the immediate care of the troops after Lord Granby, is an officer that would do great honour in any service in Europe, for his correct arrangements, good sense and discernment upon all occasions, and for a punctuality and precision which give the most entire satisfaction to all who are obliged to consult him. The reviewing generals, who inspect the army twice a year, have been selected with the greatest care, and have answered the important trust reposed in them in the most laudable manner. Their reports of the condition of the army are much more to be credited than those of Junius, whom I do advise, to atone for his shameful aspersions, by asking pardon of Lord Granby and the whole kingdom, whom he has offended by his abominable scandals. In short, to turn Junius's own battery against him, I must assert, in his own words, " that he has given strong assertions without proof, declamation without argument, and violent censures without dignity or moderation."

WILLIAM DRAPER*.

LETTER

* Sir William Draper distinguished himself last war, in the East Indies, during the siege of Madras by the French; and he commanded in chief at the taking of Manilla. When he was made a Knight of the Bath, he was so enamoured with the honour, that he had the star embroidered even on his night-gown. After his literary warfare with Junius, he went abroad on a tour through the English Colonies on the Continent of America. On the commencement of the present war, he was appointed Lieutenant Governor of Minorca, and served during the late siege of St. Philips under Lieutenant General Murray, the Governor of the Island. He has still an unsettled dispute with that officer.

A few days after his first letter to Junius, Sir William published the following curious, but well meant address to the public:

Clifton, Feb. 6, 1769.

If the voice of a well meaning individual could be heard amid the clamour, fury, and madness of the times, would it appear too rash and presumptuous to propose to the public, than an act of indemnity and oblivion may be made for all past transactions and offences, as well with respect to Mr. Wilkes as to our colonies? Such salutary expedients have been embraced by the wisest nations; such expedients have been made use of by our own, when the public confusions had arrived to some very dangerous and alarming crisis; and I believe it needs not the gift of prophecy to
foretel

LETTER III.

TO SIR WILLIAM DRAPER, KNIGHT OF
THE BATH.

SIR, 7 *February,* 1769.

YOUR defence of Lord Granby does
honour to the goodness of your heart.
You feel as you ought to do, for the reputation
of your friend, and you express yourself in the
warmest

foretel, that some such crisis is now approaching. Perhaps it will be more wise and praise-worthy to make such an act immediately, in order to prevent the possibility, not to say the probability of an insurrection at home, and in our dependencies abroad, than it will be to be obliged to have recourse to one after the mischief has been done, and the kingdom has groaned under all the miseries that avarice, ambition, hypocrisy, and madness could inflict upon it. An act of grace, indemnity, and oblivion, was passed upon the restoration of king Charles II. but I will venture to say, that had such an act been seasonably passed in the reign of his unhappy father, the civil war had been prevented, and no restoration had been necessary. It is too late to recal the messengers and edicts of wrath! Cannot the money that is now wasted in endless and mutual prosecutions, and in stopping the mouth of one man, and in opening that of another, be better employed in erecting a temple to concord? Let Mr. Wilkes lay the first stone, and such a

stone

warmest language of your passions. In any other cause, I doubt not, you would have cautiously weighed the consequences of committing your name to the licentious discourses and malignant opinions of the world. But here, I presume, you thought it would be a breach of friendship to lose one moment in consulting your understanding; as if an appeal to the public were no more than a military *coup de main*, where a brave man has no rules to follow, but the dictates of his courage. Touched with your generosity, I freely forgive the excesses into which it has led you; and, far from resenting those terms of reproach, which, considering that you are an advocate for decorum, you have heaped upon me rather too liberally, I place them to the account of an honest unreflecting indignation, in which your cooler judgment and natural politeness had no concern. I approve of the spirit, with which you have given your name

stone as I hope the builders will not refuse. May this Parliament, to use Lord Clarendon's expression, be called *The Healing Parliament!* May our foul wounds be cleansed and then closed! The English have been as famous for good-nature as for valour; let it not be said that such qualities are degenerated into savage ferocity. If any of my friends in either house of legislature shall condescend to listen to, and improve these hints, I shall think that I have not lived in vain.

WILLIAM DRAPER.

to

to the public; and, if it were a proof of any thing but spirit, I should have thought myself bound to follow your example. I should have hoped that even *my* name might carry some authority with it, if I had not seen how very little weight or consideration a printed paper receives even from the respectable signature of Sir William Draper.

You begin with a general assertion, that writers, such as I am, are the real cause of all the public evils we complain of. And do you really think, Sir William, that the licentious pen of a political writer is able to produce such important effects? A little calm reflection might have shewn you, that national calamities do not arise from the description, but from the real character and conduct of ministers. To have supported your assertion, you should have proved that the present ministry are unquestionably the *best and brightest* characters of the kingdom; and that, if the affections of the colonies have been alienated, if Corsica has been shamefully abandoned, if commerce languishes, if public credit is threatened with a new debt, and your own Manilla ransom most dishonourably given up, it has all been owing to the malice of political writers, who will not suffer the best and brightest of characters (meaning still the present ministry) to take a single

single right step for the honour or interest of the nation. But it seems you were a little tender of coming to particulars. Your conscience insinuated to you that it would be prudent to leave the characters of Grafton, North, Hillsborough, Weymouth, and Mansfield, to shift for themselves; and, truly, Sir William, the part you *have* undertaken is at least as much as you are equal to.

WITHOUT disputing Lord Granby's courage, we are yet to learn in what articles of military knowledge nature has been so very liberal to his mind. If you have served with him, you ought to have pointed out some instances of able disposition and well-concerted enterprize, which might fairly be attributed to his capacity as a general. It is you, Sir William, who make your friend appear aukward and ridiculous, by giving him a laced suit of tawdry qualifications, which nature never intended him to wear.

You say, he has acquired nothing but honour in the field. Is the Ordnance nothing? Are the Blues nothing? Is the command of the army, with all the patronage annexed to it, nothing? Where he got these *nothings* I know not; but you at least ought to have told us where he deserved them.

As

As to his bounty, compassion, &c. it would have been but little to the purpose, though you had proved all that you have asserted. I meddle with nothing but his character as commander in chief; and, though I acquit him of the baseness of selling commissions, I still assert that his military cares have never extended beyond the disposal of vacancies; and I am justified by the complaints of the whole army, when I say that, in this distribution, he consults nothing but parliamentary interests, or the gratification of his immediate dependants. As to his servile submission to the reigning ministry, let me ask, whether he did not desert the cause of the whole army, when he suffered Sir Jeffery Amherst to be sacrificed, and what share he had in recalling that officer to the service? Did he not betray the just interest of the army, in permitting Lord Percy to have a regiment? And does he not at this moment give up all character and dignity as a gentleman, in receding from his own repeated declarations in favour of Mr. Wilkes?

In the two next articles I think we are agreed. You candidly admit, that he often makes such promises as it is a virtue in him to violate, and that no man is more assiduous to provide for his relations at the public expence. I did not urge the last as an absolute vice in his difpofition, but to prove that a *carelefs difinterefted fpirit* is no part of his character; and as to the other, I defire it may be remembered, that *I* never defcended to the indecency of enquiring into his *convivial hours*. It is you, Sir William Draper, who have taken pains to reprefent your friend in the character of a drunken landlord, who deals out his promifes as liberally as his liquor, and will fuffer no man to leave his table either forrowful or fober. None but an intimate friend, who muft frequently have feen him in thefe unhappy, difgraceful moments could have defcribed him fo well.

The laft charge, of the neglect of the army, is indeed the moft material of all. I am forry to tell you, Sir William, that, in this article, your firft fact is falfe, and as there is nothing more painful to me than to give a direct contradiction to a gentleman of your appearance, I could wifh that, in your future publications, you would pay a greater attention to the truth of your premifes, before you fuffer your genius to hurry you to a conclufion. Lord Ligonier *did not* deliver the army (which you, in claffical language, are pleafed to call a palladium) into Lord Granby's hands. It was taken from him much againft his inclination, fome two or three years before Lord Granby was commander

mander in chief. As to the state of the army, I should be glad to know where you have received your intelligence. Was it in the rooms at Bath, or at your retreat at Clifton? The reports of reviewing generals comprehend only a few regiments in England, which, as they are immediately under the royal inspection, are perhaps in some tolerable order. But do you know any thing of the troops in the West Indies, the Mediterranean, and North America, to say nothing of a whole army absolutely ruined in Ireland? Inquire a little into facts, Sir William, before you publish your next panegyric upon Lord Granby, and believe me you will find there is a fault at head-quarters, which even the acknowledged care and abilities of the adjutant general cannot correct.

PERMIT me now, Sir William, to address myself personally to you, by way of thanks for the honour of your correspondence. You are by no means undeserving of notice; and it may be of consequence even to Lord Granby to have it determined, whether or no the man, who has praised him so lavishly, be himself deserving of praise. When you returned to Europe, you zealously undertook the cause of that gallant army, by whose bravery at Manilla your own fortune had been established. You complained, you threatened, you even appealed to the public in print. By what accident did it happen, that in the midst of all this bustle, and all these clamours for justice to your injured troops, the name of the Manilla ransom was suddenly buried in a profound, and, since that time, an uninterrupted silence? Did the Ministry suggest any motives to you strong enough to tempt a man of honour to desert and betray the cause of his fellow-soldiers? Was it that blushing ribband, which is now the perpetual ornament of your person? Or was it that regiment, which you afterwards (a thing unprecedented among soldiers) sold to colonel Gisborne? Or was it that government, the full pay of which you are contented to hold, with the half-pay of an Irish colonel? And do you now, after a retreat not very like that of Scipio, presume to intrude yourself, unthought-of, uncalled for, upon the patience of the public? Are your flatteries of the commander in chief directed to another regiment, which you may again dispose of on the same honourable terms? We know your prudence, Sir William, and I should be sorry to stop your preferment.

JUNIUS.

LETTER IV.

TO JUNIUS.

SIR,   17 *February* 1769.

I RECEIVED Junius's favour last night; he is determined to keep his advantage by the help of his mask; it is an excellent protection, it has saved many a man from an untimely end. But whenever he will be honest enough to lay it aside, avow himself, and produce the face which has so long lurked behind it, the world will be able to judge of his motives for writing such infamous invectives. His real name will discover his freedom and independency, or his servility to a faction. Disappointed ambition, resentment for defeated hopes, and desire of revenge, assume but too often the appearance of public spirit; but be his designs wicked or charitable, Junius should learn that it is possible to condemn measures, without a barbarous and criminal outrage against men. Junius delights to mangle carcases with a hatchet; his language and instrument have a great connexion with Clare Market, and, to do him justice, he handles his weapon most admirably. One would imagine he had been taught to throw it by the savages of America. It is therefore high time for me to step in once more to shield my friend from this merciless weapon, although I may be wounded in the attempt. But I must first ask Junius by what forced analogy and construction the moments of convivial mirth are made to signify indecency, a violation of engagements, a drunken landlord, and a desire that every one in company should be drunk likewise? He must have culled all the flowers of St. Giles's and Billingsgate to have produced such a piece of oratory. Here the hatchet descends with tenfold vengeance; but, alas! it hurts no one but its master! For Junius must not think to put words into my mouth, that seem too foul even for his own.

My friend's political engagements I know not, so cannot pretend to explain them, or assert their consistency. I know not whether Junius be considerable enough to belong to any party; if he should be so, can he affirm that he has always adhered to one set of men and measures? Is he sure that he has never sided with those whom he was first hired to abuse? Has he never abused those he was hired to praise? To say the truth, most men's politics sit much too loosely about them. But as my friend's military character was

the

the chief object that engaged me in this controversy, to that I shall return.

Junius asks what instances my friend has given of his military skill and capacity as a general? When and where he gained his honour? When he deserved his emoluments? The united voice of the army which served under him, the glorious testimony of prince Ferdinand, and of vanquished enemies, all Germany will tell him. Junius repeats the complaints of the army against parliamentary influence. I love the army too well, not to wish that such influence were less. Let Junius point out the time when it has not prevailed. It was of the least force in the time of that great man, the late duke of Cumberland, who, as a prince of the blood, was able as well as willing to stem a torrent which would have overborne any private subject. In time of war this influence is small. In peace, when discontent and faction have the surest means to operate, especially in this country, and when, from a scarcity of public spirit, the wheels of government are rarely moved, but by the power and force of obligations, its weight is always too great. Yet, if this influence at present has done no greater harm than the placing Earl Percy at the head of a regiment, I do not think that either the rights or best interests of the army are sacrificed and betrayed,

betrayed, or the nation undone. Let me afk Junius, if he knows any one nobleman in the army, who has had a regiment by feniority? I feel myfelf happy in feeing young noblemen of illuftrious name and great property come among us. They are an additional fecurity to the kingdom from foreign or domeftic flavery. Junius needs not be told, that fhould the time ever come, when this nation is to be defended only by thofe, who have nothing more to lofe than their arms and their pay, its danger will be great indeed. A happy mixture of men of quality with foldiers of fortune is always to be wifhed for. But the main point is ftill to be contended for, I mean the difcipline and condition of the army, and I muft ftill maintain, though contradicted by Junius, that it was never upon a more refpectable footing, as to all the effentials that can form good foldiers, than it is at prefent. Junius is forced to allow that our army at home may be in fome tolerable order; yet how kindly does he invite our late enemies to the invafion of Ireland, by affuring them that the army in that kingdom is totally ruined! (The colonels of that army are much obliged to him) I have too great an opinion of the military talents of the lord lieutenant, and of all their diligence and capacity, to believe it. If from fome ftrange, unaccountable fatality, the people of that kingdom

kingdom cannot be induced to confult their own fecurity, by fuch an effectual augmentation, as may enable the troops there to act with power and energy, is the commander in chief here to blame? Or is he to blame, becaufe the troops in the Mediterranean, in the Weft-Indies, in America, labour under great difficulties from the fcarcity of men, which is but too vifible all over thefe kingdoms! Many of our forces are in climates unfavourable to Britifh conftitutions: their lofs is in proportion. Britain muft recruit all thefe regiments from her own emaciated bofom, or more precarioufly, by catholicks from Ireland. We are likewife fubject to the fatal drains to the Eaft-Indies, to Senegal, and the alarming emigrations of our people to other countries: Such depopulation can only be repaired by a long peace, or by fome fenfible bill of naturalization.

I must now take the liberty to talk to Junius on my own account. He is pleafed to tell me that he addreffes himfelf to me *perfonally*, I fhall be glad to fee him. It is his *imperfonality* that I complain of, and his invifible attacks; for his dagger in the air is only to be regarded, becaufe one cannot fee the hand which holds it; but had it not wounded other people more deeply than myfelf,

felf, I should not have obtruded myfelf at all on the patience of the public.

Mark how a plain tale fhall put him down, and transfufe the blufh of my ribband into his own cheeks. Junius tells me, that at my return, I zealoufly undertook the caufe of the gallant army, by whofe bravery at Manilla my own fortunes were eftablifhed; that I complained, that I even appealed to the public. I did fo; I glory in having done fo, as I had an undoubted right to vindicate my own character, attacked by a Spanifh memorial, and to affert the rights of my brave companions. I glory likewife, that I have never taken up my pen, but to vindicate the injured. Junius afks by what accident did it happen, that in the midft of all this buftle, and all the clamours for juftice to the injured troops, the Manilla ranfom was fuddenly buried in a profound, and, fince that time, an uninterrupted filence? I will explain the caufe to the public. The feveral minifters who have been employed fince that time have been very defirous to do juftice from two moft laudable motives, a ftrong inclination to affift injured bravery, and to acquire a well deferved popularity to themfelves. Their efforts have been in vain. Some were ingenuous enough to own, that they could not think of involving this diftreffed nation into another

another war for our private concerns. In short, our rights for the present are sacrificed to national convenience; and I must confess, that although I may lose five-and-twenty thousand pounds by their acquiescence to this breach of faith in the Spaniards, I think they are in the right to temporize, considering the critical situation of this country, convulsed in every part by poison infused by anonymous, wicked, and incendiary writers. Lord Shelburne will do me the justice to own, that, in September last, I waited upon him with a joint memorial from the admiral Sir S. Cornish and myself, in behalf of our injured companions. His lordship was as frank upon the occasion as other secretaries had been before him. He did not deceive us by giving any immediate hopes of relief.

JUNIUS would basely insinuate, that my silence may have been purchased by my government, by my *blushing* ribband, by my regiment, by the sale of that regiment, and by half-pay as an Irish colonel.

HIS Majesty was pleased to give me my government, for my service at Madras. I had my first regiment in 1757. Upon my return from Manilla, his Majesty, by Lord Egremont, informed me, that I should have the first vacant red ribband, as a reward for

many

many services in an enterprize, which I had planned as well as executed. The Duke of Bedford and Mr. Grenville confirmed those assurances many months before the Spaniards had protested the ransom bills. To accommodate Lord Clive, then going upon a most important service to Bengal, I waved my claim to the vacancy which then happened. As there was no other vacancy until the Duke of Grafton and Lord Rockingham were joint ministers, I was then honoured with the order, and it is surely no small honour to me, that in such a succession of ministers, they were all pleased to think that I had deserved it; in my favour they were all united. Upon the reduction of the 79th regiment, which had served so gloriously in the East-Indies, his Majesty, unsolicited by me, gave me the 16th of foot as an equivalent. My motives for retiring afterwards are foreign to the purpose; let it suffice, that his Majesty was pleased to approve of them; they are such as no man can think indecent, who knows the shocks that repeated vicissitudes of heat and cold, of dangerous and sickly climates, will give to the best constitutions in a pretty long course of service. I resigned my regiment to colonel Gisborne, a very good officer, for his half-pay, 1200l. Irish annuity; so that, according to Junius, I have been bribed to say nothing more of the Manilla

nilla ranfom, and facrifice thofe brave men by the ftrange avarice of accepting three hundred and eighty pounds per ann. and giving up eight hundred! If this be bribery, it is not the bribery of thefe times. As to my flattery, thofe who know me will judge of it. By the afperity of Junius's ftile, I cannot indeed call him a flatterer, unlefs he be as a cynick or a maftiff: if he wags his tail, he will ftill growl, and long to bite. The public will now judge of the credit that ought to be given to Junius's writings, from the falfities that he has infinuated with refpect to myfelf.

WILLIAM DRAPER.

LETTER V.

TO SIR WILLIAM DRAPER, KNIGHT OF THE BATH.

SIR, 21 *February*, 1769.

I SHOULD juftly be fufpected of acting upon motives of more than common enmity to Lord Granby, if I continued to give you frefh materials or occafion for writing in his defence. Individuals who hate, and the public who defpife, have read *your* letters, Sir William, with infinitely more fatisfaction than mine. Unfortunately

for

for him, his reputation, like that unhappy country to which you refer me for his last military atchievements, has suffered more by his friends than his enemies. In mercy to him, let us drop the subject. For my own part, I willingly leave it to the public to determine whether your vindication of your friend has been as able and judicious, as it was certainly well intended; and you, I think, may be satisfied with the warm acknowledgements he already owes you, for making him the principal figure in a piece, in which, but for your amicable assistance, he might have passed without particular notice or distinction.

In justice to your friends, let your future labours be confined to the care of your own reputation. Your declaration, that you are happy in seeing young noblemen *come among us*, is liable to two objections. With respect to Lord Percy, it means nothing, for he was already in the army. He was aid de camp to the King, and had the rank of colonel. A regiment therefore could not make him a more military man, though it made him richer, and probably at the expence of some brave, deserving, friendless officer.—The other concerns yourself. After selling the companions of your victory in one instance, and after selling your profession in the other,

by

by what authority do you presume to call yourself a soldier? The plain evidence of facts is superior to all declarations. Before you were appointed to the 16th regiment, your complaints were a distress to government;—from that moment you were silent. The conclusion is inevitable. You insinuate to us that your ill state of health obliged you to quit the service. The retirement necessary to repair a broken constitution would have been as good a reason for not accepting, as for resigning the command of a regiment. There is certainly an error of the press, or an affected obscurity in that paragraph, where you speak of your bargain with colonel Gisborne. Instead of attempting to answer what I do not really understand, permit me to explain to the public what I really know. In exchange for your regiment, you accepted of a colonel's half-pay (at least 220l. a year) and an annuity of 200l. for your own and lady Draper's life jointly.—And is this the losing bargain, which you would represent to us, as if you had given up an income of 800l. a year for 380l.? Was it decent, was it honourable, in a man, who pretends to love the army, and calls himself a soldier, to make a traffic of the royal favour, and turn the highest honour of an active profession into a sordid provision for himself and his family? It were unworthy of me to press you farther.

The

The contempt with which the whole army heard of the manner of your retreat, assures me, that as your conduct was not justified by precedent, it will never be thought an example for imitation.

The last and most important question remains. When you receive your half-pay, do you, or do you not, take a solemn oath, or sign a declaration upon your honour, to the following effect? *That you do not actually hold any place of profit, civil or military, under his Majesty.* The charge which the question plainly conveys against you, is of so shocking a complection, that I sincerely wish you may be able to answer it well, not merely for the colour of your reputation, but for your own inward peace of mind.

JUNIUS.

LETTER VI.

TO JUNIUS.

SIR, 27 *February*, 1769.

I HAVE a very short answer for Junius's important question: I do not either take an oath, or declare upon honour, that I have no *place* of profit, *civil* or military, when

when I receive the half-pay as an Irish colonel. My most gracious Sovereign gives it me as a penſion: he was pleaſed to think I deſerved it. The annuity of 200l. Iriſh, and the equivalent for the half-pay together, produces no more than 380l. per annum, clear of fees and perquiſites of office. I receive 167l. from my government of Yarmouth. Total 547l. per annum. My conſcience is much at eaſe in theſe particulars; my friends need not bluſh for me.

Junius makes much and frequent uſe of interrogations: they are arms that may be eaſily turned againſt himſelf. I could, by malicious interrogation, diſturb the peace of the moſt virtuous man in the kingdom; I could take the decalogue, and ſay to one man, Did you never ſteal? To the next, Did you never commit murder? And to Junius himſelf, who is putting my life and conduct to the rack, Did you never bear falſe witneſs againſt thy neighbour? Junius muſt eaſily ſee, that unleſs he affirms to the contrary, in his real name, ſome people who may be as ignorant of him as I am, will be apt to ſuſpect him of having deviated a little from the truth: therefore let Junius aſk no more queſtions. You bite againſt a file: ceaſe viper.

LET-

LETTER VII.

TO SIR WILLIAM DRAPER, KNIGHT OF
THE BATH.

SIR, 3 *March*, 1769.

AN academical education has given you an unlimited command over the most beautiful figures of speech. Masks, hatchets, racks, and vipers dance through your letters in all the mazes of metaphorical confusion. These are the gloomy companions of a disturbed imagination; the melancholy madness of poetry, without the inspiration. I will not contend with you in point of composition. You are a scholar, Sir William, and if I am truly informed, you write Latin with almost as much purity as English. Suffer me then, for I am a plain unlettered man, to continue that stile of interrogation, which suits my capacity, and to which, considering the readiness of your answers, you ought to have no objection. Even * Mr.

---

* BINGLEY was committed by the King's Bench for a contempt of court, on which he made a voluntary oath, that he would not answer interrogatories, unless he was put to the torture.

Bingley

Bingley promises to answer, if put to the torture.

Do you then really think that, if I were to ask a *most virtuous man* whether he ever committed theft, or murder, it would disturb his peace of mind? Such a question might perhaps discompose the gravity of his muscles, but I believe it would little affect the tranquility of his conscience. Examine your own breast, Sir William, and you will discover, that reproaches and enquiries have no power to afflict either the man of unblemished integrity, or the abandoned profligate. It is the middle compound character which alone is vulnerable: the man, who, without firmness enough to avoid a dishonourable action, has feeling enough to be ashamed of it.

I THANK you for the hint of the decalogue, and shall take an opportunity of applying it to some of your most virtuous friends in both houses of parliament.

You seem to have dropped the affair of your regiment; so let it rest. When you are appointed to another, I dare say you will not sell it either for a gross sum or for an annuity upon lives.

I AM truly glad (for really, Sir William, I am not your enemy, nor did I begin this contest with you) that you have been able to clear yourself of a crime, though at the expence of the highest indiscretion. You say that your half-pay was given you by way of pension. I will not dwell upon the singularity of uniting in your own person two sorts of provision, which in their own nature, and in all military and parliamentary views, are incompatible; but I call upon you to justify that declaration, wherein you charge your Sovereign with having done an act in your favour notoriously against law. The half-pay, both in Ireland and England, is appropriated by parliament; and if it be given to persons, who, like you, are legally incapable of holding it, it is a breach of law. It would have been more decent in you to have called this dishonourable transaction by its true name; a job to accommodate two persons, by particular interest and management at the castle. What sense must government have had of your services, when the rewards they have given you are only a disgrace to you!

AND now, Sir William, I shall take my leave of you for ever. Motives very different from any apprehension of your resentment, make it impossible you should ever know

know me. In truth, you have some reason to hold yourself indebted to me. From the lessons I have given you, you may collect a profitable instruction for your future life. They will either teach you so to regulate your conduct, as to be able to set the most malicious inquiries at defiance; or, if that be a lost hope, they will teach you prudence enough not to attract the public attention to a character, which will only pass without censure, when it passes without observation*.

* Sir William Draper's interference occasioned the Marquis of Granby's character to be more enlarged upon than was at first intended. The contest, for the present, closed with this letter, the Marquis having signified to Sir William to desist writing in his defence. On Wednesday the 17th of January 1770, the Marquis resigned all his places, except the Blues, and condemned openly in the House of Commons that political system, which had drawn on him the notice of Junius. He died in October, the same year, universally lamented.

LETTER VIII.

TO THE DUKE OF GRAFTON.

MY LORD,   18 *March*, 1769.

BEFORE you were placed at the head of affairs, it had been a maxim of the English government, not unwillingly admitted by the people, that every ungracious or severe exertion of the prerogative should be placed to the account of the Minister; but that, whenever an act of grace or benevolence was to be performed, the whole merit of it should be attributed to the Sovereign himself. It was a wise doctrine, my Lord, and equally advantageous to the King and his subjects; for while it preserved that suspicious attention with which the people ought always to examine the conduct of ministers, it tended at the same time rather to increase than diminish their attachment to the person of their Sovereign. If there be not a fatality attending every measure you are concerned in, by what treachery, or by what excess of folly has it happened, that those ungracious acts, which have distinguished your administration, and which I doubt not were entirely your own, should carry with them a strong appearance of personal interest, and even of personal enmity in a quarter, where no such interest or enmity can be supposed to exist, without the highest injustice and the highest dishonour? On the other hand, by what judicious management have you contrived it, that the only act of mercy, to which you ever advised your Sovereign, far from adding to the lustre of a character, truly gracious and benevolent, should be received with universal disapprobation and disgust? I shall consider it as a ministerial measure, because it is an odious one, and as your measure, my Lord Duke, because you are the minister.

As long as the trial of this chairman was depending, it was natural enough that government should give him every possible encouragement and support. The honourable service for which he was hired, and the spirit with which he performed it, made common cause between your grace and him. The minister, who by secret corruption invades the freedom of elections, and the ruffian, who by open violence destroys that freedom, are embarked in the same bottom. They have the same interests, and mutually feel for each other. To do justice to your Grace's humanity, you felt for MacQuirk as you ought to do, and if you had been contented to affift him indirectly, without a notorious denial of juftice, or openly infulting the fenfe of the nation, you might have fatisfied every duty of political friendfhip, without committing the honour of your Sovereign, or hazarding the reputation of his government. But when this unhappy man had been folemnly tried, convicted and condemned;—when it appeared that he had been frequently employed in the fame services, and that no excufe for him could be drawn either from the innocence of his former life, or the fimplicity of his character, was it not hazarding too much to interpofe the ftrength of the prerogative between this felon and the juftice of his country*? You ought to

---

* *Whitehall, March* 11, 1769. His Majefty has been gracioufly pleafed to extend his royal mercy to Edward M'Quirk, found guilty of the murder of George Clarke, as appears by his royal warrant to the tenor following.

GEORGE R.

WHEREAS a doubt had arifen in Our Royal breaft concerning the evidence of the death of George Clarke, from the reprefentations of William Bromfield, Efq; Surgeon, and Solomon Starling, Apothecary; both of whom, as has been reprefented to Us, attended the deceafed before his death, and expreffed their opinions that he did not die of the blow he received at Brentford: And whereas it appears to Us, that neither of the faid perfons were produced as witneffes upon the trial, though the
said

to have known that an example of this sort was never so necessary as at present; and certainly you must have known that the lot could not have fallen upon a more guilty object.

said Solomon Starling had been examined before the Coroner, and the only person called to prove that the death of the said George Clarke was occasioned by the said blow, was John Foot, Surgeon, who never saw the deceased till after his death; We thought fit thereupon to refer the said representations, together with the report of the Recorder of Our city of London, of the evidence given by Richard and William Beale, and the said John Foot, on the trial of Edward Quirk, otherwise called Edward Kirk, otherwise called Edward M'Quirk, for the murder of the said Clark, to the master, wardens, and the rest of the court of examiners of the Surgeons company, commanding them likewise to take such further examination of the said persons so representing, and of said John Foot, as they might think necessary, together with the premises abovementioned, to form and report to Us their opinion, " Whether it did or did not appear to " them, that the said George Clarke died in consequence " of the blow he received in the riot at Brentford on " the 8th of December last." And the said court of examiners of the Surgeons company having thereupon reported to Us their opinion, " That it did not appear to " them that he did;" We have thought proper to extend Our royal mercy to him the said Edward Quirk, otherwise called Edward Kirk, otherwise called Edward M'Quirk, and to grant him our free pardon for the Murder of the said George Clarke, of which he has been found guilty: Our will and pleasure therefore is, That he the said Edward Quirk, otherwise called Edward Kirk, otherwise called Edward M'Quirk, be inserted, for the said Murder

object. What system of government is this? You are perpetually complaining of the riotous disposition of the lower class of people, yet when the laws have given you the means of making an example, in every sense unexceptionable, and by far the most likely to awe the multitude, you pardon the offence, and are not ashamed to give the sanction of government to the riots you complain of, and even to future murders. You are partial perhaps to the military mode of execution, and had rather see a score of these wretches butchered by the guards, than one of them suffer death by regular course of law. How does it happen, my Lord, that in *your* hands, even the mercy of the prerogative is cruelty and oppression to the subject?

der, in Our first and next general pardon that shall come out for the poor convicts of Newgate, without any condition whatsoever; and that in the mean time you take bail for his appearance, in order to plead Our said pardon. And for so doing this shall be your warrant.

Given at Our court at St. James's the 10th day of March, 1769, in the ninth year of Our reign.
By his Majesty's command,
ROCHFORD.

To our trusty and well beloved James Eyre, Esq; Recorder of Our city of London, the Sheriffs of Our said city and county of Middlesex, and all others whom it may concern.

THE

The measure it seems was so extraordinary, that you thought it necessary to give some reasons for it to the public. Let them be fairly examined.

1. You say *that Messrs: Bromfield and Starling were not examined at MacQuirk's trial.* I will tell your Grace why they were not. They must have been examined upon oath; and it was foreseen, that their evidence would either not benefit, or might be prejudicial to the prisoner. Otherwise, is it conceivable that his counsel should neglect to call in such material evidence.

You say that *Mr. Foot did not see the deceased until after his death.* A surgeon, my Lord, must know very little of his profession, if, upon examining a wound, or a contusion, he cannot determine whether it was mortal or not.—While the party is alive, a surgeon will be cautious of pronouncing; whereas by the death of the patient, he is enabled to consider both cause and effect in one view, and to speak with a certainty confirmed by experience.

YET we are to thank your Grace for the establishment of a new tribunal. Your *inquisitio post mortem* is unknown to the laws of England, and does honour to your invention.

The only material objection to it is, that if Mr. Foot's evidence was infufficient, becaufe he did not examine the wound till after the death of the party, much lefs can a negative opinion, given by gentlemen who never faw the body of Mr. Clarke, either before or after his deceafe, authorife you to fuperfede the verdict of a jury, and the fentence of the law.

Now, my Lord, let me afk you, Has it never occurred to your Grace, while you were withdrawing this defperate wretch from that juftice which the laws had awarded, and which the whole people of England demanded againft him, that there is another man, who is the favourite of his country, whofe pardon would have been accepted with gratitude, whofe pardon would have healed all our divifions? Have you quite forgotten that this man was once your Grace's friend? Or is it to murderers only that you will extend the mercy of the crown.

THESE are queftions you will not anfwer. Nor is it neceffary. The character of your private life, and the uniform tenour of your public conduct, is an anfwer to them all.

JUNIUS.

LETTER IX.

A VINDICATION OF THE DUKE OF GRAFTON, IN ANSWER TO A LETTER SIGNED JUNIUS.

THE foregoing letter of Junius addressed to the Duke of Grafton, produced a vindication of his Grace in a pamphlet of forty-seven pages, by one who calls himself, *A Volunteer in the Service of Government,* and takes God to witness that neither his Grace, nor any other servant of the crown has the least intimation or knowledge of it. This gentleman has entered fully into the merits of the complaint; and has, he thinks, exposed the wit, sophistry, and malice of Junius, with common sense, truth, and good nature.

The maxim, he says, of English government, (that the king can do no wrong) of which Junius endeavours to pervert the sense, owes its birth to a catastrophe, and is adopted as a bar against a like event on a like occasion. But to say that every ungracious and severe exertion of the prerogative is to be placed to the account of the minister; and every act of grace and benevolence to that of the king, as Junius hath advanced, is as falſe as unjuſt; for it is as much the duty of a miniſter to adviſe in the latter caſe as in the former; and he is therefore entitled to ſhare in the praiſe that may reſult from the one, full as much as in the blame that may be laid on the other.

The ungracious acts of his Grace's adminiſtration, alluded to by Junius, the Volunteer ſuppoſes are:

1. That ſole mitigated act of juſtice which the firſt and moſt inſolent of all offenders of his claſs has drawn upon himſelf, and,

2. That act of mercy which Junius has made the ſubject of his abuſe.

As to the appearance of perſonal intereſt and perſonal enmity operating, in the firſt caſe, from a quarter where no ſuch intereſt or enmity can be ſuppoſed to exiſt; ſhould it be true, that the criminal has offended that quarter by the vileſt aſperſions in the moſt tender point, a point too ſacred to be recollected, and which no nation on earth, except our own, would have borne to be attempted; that to this purpoſe he had amuſed, inflamed, and bewitched the minds of the young

young and lively, by the moſt villainous and moſt infernal inuendos, ſtrictures, and interpretations, on an intercourſe which had been ſolely founded on the moſt cogent and moſt virtuous motives; under ſuch unmerited and unparalleled provocation, kings muſt either be ſuppoſed to be Gods or Brutes not to be ſuſceptible of the deepeſt impreſſions.

In the ſecond caſe, it muſt have occurred to his Grace, that the latter was an honeſt fellow in compariſon to the former. That he was a low-bred, ill-adviſed, unhappy wretch, who, from being employed by his betters, in ſeveral conteſted elections, to act according to their occaſional commands, with the utmoſt impunity, had taken it for granted, that the licentiouſneſs of an election riot was beyond the reach of the laws. That, having been intoxicated with liquor, or deceived by a ſilly or malicious prompter, or ſignal, he fancied himſelf to be called upon, to drive the adverſary from the field of conteſt. That he was but one, of many, who had been led, or had fallen into the ſame error with himſelf, and who, by laying about them like madmen, committed more miſchief than they ever intended; eſpecially, by ſtriking an unlucky blow, of which the perſon who received it was aſſerted to have died; and whoſe death,

by

by the coroner's inqueſt, was deemed wilful murder by a perſon or perſons unknown. That, notwithſtanding this verdict, the ſurgeon who had attended him before he died, had informed the Secretary of State, that he was of a very different opinion. That, moreover, the culprit was ſo little aware of having had any ſhare in that particular accident; and was ſo little aprehenſive of reſearches to be made after the individuals of an election riot, that he had not only returned to the buſineſs of his legal calling, but had had the imprudence to converſe on what he had done, with his friends and acquaintance. That having met with a perſon, who by his birth and appearance was a gentleman, and whom he had ſaved from a blow, which might have proved as fatal as the other; he had not ſcrupled to accept of his offer, of treating him with ſome liquor by way of gratitude, nor of relating to him whatever he knew of the riot, and of his own ſhare in it. That he had been ſhamefully betrayed by this pretended grateful gentleman. That he had no ſooner been made ſenſible, by his impending fate, of the unlawfulneſs and criminality of this election buſineſs, but he had cried out for mercy, with promiſes of never being guilty of the like for the future. That he had not been indicted, and condemned for murder, but for aiding and abetting in it. That theſe and many ny other circumstances did certainly plead in his favour. But then, that his trial and condemnation had been attended with circumstances on the part of the audience, which had shocked all decency and humanity; and had shown, at the same time, such a spirit of resentment and infatuation in those who had been the opponents of the candidate, whose success he had spoiled by his misconduct, as was highly and criminally reflecting on government, as if the execution of this convict was to have been a mere sacrifice to liberty, falsely pretended to be injured by government itself. That this latter was a nettling occurrence. That it was as dangerous for the ministry to abandon this poor fellow to the severity of the law, as to give way to the circumstances which pleaded for his pardon. That if he was hanged, the crafty disturbers of public tranquility would not fail to say, that the ministry had been afraid to lay his case before the King; and had sacrificed the poor fellow, to their fear of shewing him to be their own tool, by recommending him to the royal mercy. That if, on the other hand, they complied with the duties of their stations, in laying before the King, the intercessions that were made in his behalf, with the circumstances upon which they were founded; the same revilers of government would not fail to say, in case his Majesty should

should grant his pardon, that this royal act was a contrivance of their own, to save their tool from the gallows, and to bind him thereby to secrecy. That, in good policy, the latter was, however, preferable to the other. That if the man was hanged, the rascals could make him a dying speech of their own invention, pretending it to have been conveyed to them one way or other. That, on the contrary, if he was kept alive, and set at liberty, it would not be so easy for them to engage a man, who had once escaped so narrowly the power of the law, to stand the chance of being tried for perjury. But after all, that honesty was the best policy, and that therefore, the most eligible of all was, to pay no attention to whatever the malice of others, or one's own interest might suggest, but to keep up to the rules of office, as well as to those of justice and humanity; to let the applications for mercy take their natural course to the throne, full as much as those for justice had done to the bar; to let the circumstances alledged be referred to whatever persons, courts, or offices, were entitled to report on the same, and to let his Majesty determine from thence, according to the dictates of his own wisdom, justice, and clemency.

I SHALL

I SHALL, therefore, says this Volunteer, leave it to the public to judge, whether they ought not to despise, and even to detest and abhor the fascinating powers of Junius's infernal pen; and not suffer themselves to be attracted by the deceitful colour and flavour of the most subtle and penetrating poison that ever was invented, except by that arch fiend of his king and country, to whose society, and his society alone, Junius deserves to be confined for ever, by such a punishment as in justice and good policy, if not in law, ought to be inflicted on every man, whose powerful talents, of what nature soever, are only employed to the destruction of civil society, and subversion of a state.

WITH respect to Mr. Wilkes, the Volunteer acknowledges, that the Duke was one of his betters, that had once been his friend; that he had not scrupled when Secretary of State to join his purse to those of others to maintain the culprit in his own expensive way, whilst he was considered as an outlaw; but that being at last convinced of the apparent resolution of this desperate criminal, to attempt as far as he could the ruin of his country, in order to gratify his own extravagant prodigality and Catalinian ambition, he had resolved, in his turn, not only totally to abandon him to the perversity of his nature

ture, and to the tremendous confequences of his defperate conduct, but to act the part of a moſt zealous and moſt faithful fervant of the crown, of one of the guardians of the conſtitution, and of one of the reſtorers of the public tranquility, to the terror and deſtruction of this and every other feditious firebrand, who fhould continue to pervert and inflame the minds of his Majeſty's unguarded fubjects.

LETTER X.

TO HIS GRACE THE DUKE OF GRAFTON.

MY LORD,   10 *April,* 1769.

I HAVE fo good an opinion of your Grace's difcernment, that when the author of the vindication of your conduct affures us, that he writes from his own mere motion, without the leaſt authority from your Grace, I fhould be ready enough to believe him, but for one fatal mark, which feems to be fixed upon every meafure, in which either your perfonal or your political character is concerned.—Your firſt attempt to fupport Sir William Proctor ended in the election of Mr. Wilkes; the fecond enfured fuccefs to Mr. Glynn. The extraordinary
ſtep

step you took to make Sir James Lowther Lord Paramount of Cumberland, has ruined his interest in that county for ever. The House List of Directors was cursed with the concurrence of government; and even the miserable * Dingley could not escape the misfortune of your Grace's protection. With this uniform experience before us, we are authorised to suspect, that when a pretended vindication of your principles and conduct in reality contains the bitterest reflections upon both, it could not have been written without your immediate direction and assistance. The author indeed calls God to witness for him, with all the sincerity, and in the very terms of an Irish evidence, *to the best of his knowledge and belief.* My Lord, you should not encourage these appeals to heaven. The pious Prince, from whom you are supposed to descend, made such frequent use of them in his public declarations, that at last the people also found it necessary to appeal to heaven in their turn. Your administration has driven us into circumstances of equal distress;—beware at least how you remind us of the remedy.

* Mr. Dingley was persuaded by the Duke to stand candidate for Middlesex, but he could not prevail on any freeholder to put him in nomination.

You have already much to anſwer for. You have provoked this unhappy gentleman to play the fool once more in public life, in ſpite of his years and infirmities, and to ſhew us, that, as you yourſelf are a ſingular inſtance of youth without ſpirit, the man who defends you is a no leſs remarkable example of age without the benefits of experience. To follow ſuch a writer minutely would, like his own periods, be a labour without end. The ſubject too has been already diſcuſſed, and is ſufficiently underſtood. I cannot help obſerving, however, that, when the pardon of MacQuirk was the principal charge againſt you, it would have been but a decent compliment to your Grace's underſtanding, to have defended you upon your own principles. What credit does a man deſerve, who tells us plainly, that the facts ſet forth in the King's proclamation were not the true motives on which the pardon was granted, and that he wiſhes that thoſe chirurgical reports, which firſt gave occaſion to certain doubts in the royal breaſt, had not been laid before his Majeſty. You ſee, my Lord, that even your friends cannot defend your actions, without changing your principles, nor juſtify a deliberate meaſure of government, without contradicting the main aſſertion on which it was founded.

The conviction of MacQuirk had reduced you to a dilemma, in which it was hardly possible for you to reconcile your political interest with your duty. You were obliged either to abandon an active useful partisan, or to protect a felon from public justice. With your usual spirit, you preferred your interest to every other consideration; and with your usual judgment, you founded your determination upon the only motives, which should not have been given to the public.

I have frequently censured Mr. Wilkes's conduct, yet your advocate reproaches me with having devoted myself to the service of sedition. Your Grace can best inform us, for which of Mr. Wilkes's good qualities you first honoured him with your friendship, or how long it was before you discovered those bad ones in him, at which, it seems, your delicacy was offended. Remember, my Lord, that you continued your connexion with Mr. Wilkes long after he had been convicted of those crimes, which you have since taken pains to represent in the blackest colours of blasphemy and treason. How unlucky is it, that the first instance you have given us of a scrupulous regard to decorum is united with the breach of a moral obligation! For my own part, my Lord, I am proud to affirm,

affirm, that, if I had been weak enough to form such a friendship, I would never have been base enough to betray it. But, let Mr. Wilkes's character be what it may, this at least is certain, that, circumstanced as he is with regard to the public, even his vices plead for him. The people of England have too much discernment to suffer your Grace to take advantage of the failings of a private character, to establish a precedent by which the public liberty is affected, and which you may hereafter, with equal ease and satisfaction, employ to the ruin of the best men in the kingdom.——Content yourself, my Lord, with the many advantages, which the unsullied purity of your own character has given you over your unhappy deserted friend. Avail yourself of all the unforgiving piety of the court you live in, and bless God that you " are not as " other men are; extortioners, unjust, adul- " terers, or even as this publican." In a heart void of feeling, the laws of honour and good faith may be violated with impunity, and there you may safely indulge your genius. But the laws of England shall not be violated, even by your holy zeal to oppress a sinner; and though you have succeeded in making him a tool, you shall not make him the victim of your ambition.

JUNIUS.

LETTER XI.

REPLY TO THE ABOVE LETTER BY THE VOLUNTEER.

SHOULD I be so unlucky, says he, not to have defended your Grace on your own principles, it should not be for mine, but for your own, and the public's sake, that I should be sorry. But this pretension of Master Junius is too fallacious to be dwelt upon; and I shall trust to the steadiness of your Grace's public conduct to give him the lie in this respect. In the mean while I shall do so here, in vindication of my own veracity, and to clear myself of his false and impudent assertion of my having told plainly, " that the facts set forth in the king's proclamation were not the true motives on which the pardon was granted." To say that I have directly or indirectly told this, is as gross a lie as he or any man ever uttered. I have indeed told the public, and I repeat it here, that I could not but regret that the Earl of Rochford, whether with, or without the concurrence of his co-ministers, seemed to have thought proper to lay the chirurgical reports before the king in preference to all the other sufficient motives that were alledged, and

and were, or might have been suggested to his majesty in behalf of the pardoned convict. But this implies in the fullest manner, that the pardon was granted by the king, in consequence of those reports, as it was set forth in the proclamation. And as to the consequence which Junius draws from his lie, the latter part vanishes with it, and the other shews him to be as void of logic as of truth; for what has the mode of an action to do with its principle. I suppose for a moment that your Grace had a mind, from a due regard to justice and the public safety, to get this Junius punished according to his desert, would it change your principle, whether you thought proper to have it done by a horse-whip, by an axe, or by an halter? No more, I hope, my Lord Duke, could it change the principle of justice and humanity, on which you advised the pardon of M'Quirk, whether it was done with laying before the king any other circumstance which pleaded in his favour, or that of the chirurgical opinions and reports.

LETTER XII.

TO MR. EDWARD WESTON.*

SIR,   21 *April,* 1769.

I SAID you were an old man without the benefit of experience. It seems you are also a volunteer with the stipend of twenty commissions; and at a period when all prospects are at an end, you are still looking forward to rewards, which you cannot enjoy. No man is better acquainted with the bounty of government than you are.

   ———*ton impudence,*
   Temeraire vieillard, aura sa recompense.

---

* A privy counsellor in Ireland, writer of the Gazette, comptroller of the salt office, one of the chief clerks of the signet, and a pensioner on the Irish establishment. A charge was brought against him in the news papers, that when he was under Secretary of State, the division of 500l. among ten people was left to his discretion, 400l. of which he modestly claimed for his own share. Such is this volunteer! the volunteer, to this charge, confesses that he knows Mr. Weston, but declares upon his honour, that the Right Hon. Mr. Weston has never had the least share in, or knowledge of this vindication of the Duke of Grafton; and as to his claim of 400l. out of 500l. he is sure it must be a downright lie, or a gross misrepresentation.

But I will not descend to an altercation either with the impotence of your age, or the peevishness of your diseases. Your pamphlet, ingenious as it is, has been so little read, that the public cannot know how far you have a right to give me the lye, without the following citation of your own words.

Page 6—' 1. That he is persuaded that
' the motives, which he (Mr. Weston) has
' alledged, must appear fully sufficient, with
' or without the opinions of the surgeons.

' That those very motives MUST HAVE
' BEEN the foundation, on which the Earl of
' Rochford thought proper, &c.

' That he CANNOT BUT REGRET that
' the Earl of Rochford seems to have thought
' proper to lay the chirurgical reports before
' the king, in preference to all the other suf-
' ficient motives,' &c.

Let the public determine whether this be defending government on their principles or your own.

The style and language you have adopted are, I confess, not ill suited to the elegance of your own manners, or to the dignity of the cause you have undertaken. Every common
dauber

dauber writes rascal and villain under his pictures, becaufe the pictures themfelves have neither character nor refemblance. But the works of a mafter require no index. His features and colouring are taken from nature. The impreffion they make is immediate and uniform ; nor is it poffible to miftake his characters, whether they reprefent the treachery of a minifter, or the abufed fimplicity of a ———*.

JUNIUS.

A MONODY. XIII.

OR THE TEARS OF SEDITION ON THE DEATH OF JUNIUS.

Quis tibi Silure furor ?

AND are thofe periods fill'd with tuneful care,
   Thofe thoughts which gleam'd with Ciceronian ore,
Are they, my Junius, pafs'd like vulgar air,
   Droop'd is thy plume, to rife on fame no more?

Thy plume!—it was the harp of fong in profe :
   Oft have its numbers footh'd the felon's ear,

---

* The word " *king*" was left blank in the original publication.

Oft to it's tune my Wilkite heroes rose
  With couch'd tobacco pipes in act to spear.

Where now shall stormy Clodius and his crew,
  My dear assembly to the midnight hour,
Ah! where acquire a trumpeter?—since you
  No more shall rouze them with your classic
    power.

Accurs'd * Silerus! blasted be thy wing!
  That grey Scotch wing which led th' uner-
    ring dart!
In virtue's cause could all that's satire sting
  A bosom with corruption's poison fraught!

Impossible!—then hear me, fiends of Hell,
  This dark event, this mystery unfold;
Poison'd was Junius? No; " Alas, he fell,
  " 'Midst arrows dipp'd in ministerial gold."

Then hear me, rioters, of my command,
  Condemn the villain to a traitor's doom;
Let none but faithful knaves adorn my band;
  Go, sink this character into his tomb.

Here sunk an essayist of dubious name,
  Whose tinsel'd page on airy cadence run,
Friendless, with party—noted without fame,
  Virtue and vice disclaim'd him as a son.
                    POETICASTOS.

   * A writer in opposition to Wilkes.
                                    This

This little piece produced the following remarkable explanations.

LETTER XIV.

TO POETICASTOS.

THE Monody on the suppoſed death of Junius is not leſs poetical for being founded on a fiction. In ſome parts of it, there is a promiſe of genius, which deſerves to be encouraged. My letter of Monday [April 10,] will, I hope, convince the author that I am neither a partizan of Mr. Wilkes, nor yet bought off by the miniſtry. It is true I have refuſed offers, which a more prudent or a more intereſted man would have accepted. Whether it be ſimplicity or virtue in me, I can only affirm that I am in earneſt; becauſe I am convinced, as far as my underſtanding is capable of judging, that the preſent miniſtry is driving this country to deſtruction; and you, I think Sir, may be ſatisfied that my rank and fortune place me above a common bribe.

JUNIUS.

A CARD. XV.

TO JUNIUS.

POETICASTOS prefents his compliments to Junius, and is glad to underſtand from ſo celebrated a judge of the beautiful and ſublime, that there is " a promiſe of genius" in his Monody. He could wiſh that it were in his power, either as a man of taſte or honour, to pay Junius any return of praiſe: as the motive and manner of the Eſſayiſt deprive Poeticaſtos of this power, he muſt take the liberty of cautioning him never to expoſe himſelf ſo far again, as to make a line of doggrel the ſuppoſed cauſe of announcing his fictitious importance to the public.

IF Junius dares to be ſincere, inſtead of being in earneſt, let him point out the deſtruction to which the miniſters are driving this country, in a more rational and gentlemanlike manner than that ill-bred and cowardly method in which he would ſtain the perſonal honour of the miniſter, without being able to detract from the propriety of his meaſures.

LET him not hint at the offers which he had not the prudence to accept,—let him publiſh

publish them particularly and expressly. Let him not ask for an uncommon bribe on account of a supposed rank and fortune, or assert, in childish terms, that he is not a partisan of Mr. Wilkes, but let the spirit of his writing shew, that he is neither a hungry traducer of the merits of character, nor the hireling of the most contemptible of parties.

POETICASTOS will then, and not till then, have so favourable an idea of Junius, as to give him some credit—he will perhaps offer him some more poetical compositions, and be desirous of a personal acquaintance with a reformed or undeceived imitator of a TULLY.

LETTER XVI.

TO JUNIUS.

I ALWAYS suspected your honesty. You have now convinced me of your cowardice. Unable and afraid to answer a charge of dishonour brought publicly against you in the language of resolution, you now begin to crow over the infirmities of a man confessedly incapable of chastising your insolence in any respect. Is, Sir, the public to be abused any longer with your scandalous impositions? Or how dare you to pretend, after swallowing a lye like a scoundrel, to appear again before the world, as if you could merit attention? But you would offer the judgment of the nation a more glaring affront; you would give a blustering air of resolution to the timid baseness of your heart, by daring to speak treason in a manner that you are sure of escaping. To day you conclude your despicable vindication of an honour which you do not possess, by asserting " that you are a master in the art of representing the treachery of the minister, and the abused simplicity of a ————." Villain! of whom? Dare to fill the blank! but you say it is unnecessary.—Every man in the kingdom understands you. If they do, I appeal to them what punishment you merit; and if the law will not inflict it, I will, if you have the shadow of sensibility. You who write under the name of Junius, are a base scoundrel; you lye, and you may find out who gives you the lye. If you dare to appear in this paper again, without an apology for your conduct, I will convince you I am not ignorant of your person and residence.

POETICASTOS.

To this several answers appeared, but the following bears the true spirit of Junius.

LETTER

LETTER XVII.

TO POETICASTOS.

SIR,

POETICASTOS in his letter to Junius, is in such a violent rage, that he forgets to sign his real name. The *blood and thunder*, the *storming, ranting*, and *blustering* in his short epistle could have come from none but Drawcansir himself. He grows raving mad at the following extract which he quotes from Junius's letter, viz. that he is a " master in the art of representing the trea-" chery of the minister, and the abused " simplicity of a ———;" and then follows the word villain, and in so ambiguous a manner, that many readers are in doubt whether it is not intended to fill up the ———, and to prepare the challenge that follows. Now, Sir, whether Drawcansir intended it or not, or whether Junius will accept his challenge or not, I am determined to meet him whenever he chooses it; and if he is a Scotchman, I will smother him in his own brimstone; if a Welchman, hur shall eat hur own leeks; if Irish, he shall chew potatoes from the mouth of my pistol; and for this infamous way of filling up the blanks in Junius's letter, he shall no longer fill another blank in the creation.

HECTOR.

A CARD XVIII.

POETICASTOS presents his compliments to the redoubtable supporters of the Bill of Rights, and returns them a thousand thanks for the use which he had ventured to take of their new method of overcoming enemies without spilling of blood, and of acquiring laurels without moving from the tavern. He takes the liberty, as they have given no name to that new engine with which they have overset the Coventry addressers, to bestow on it the title of the Patriotic Blunderbuss, and fires it thus upon his dreadful adversary, Junius, Hector, and Crito, in one person.

Bedlam, April 27, 1769.

Poeticastos in his chair.

Resolved, That the Adviser, Author, and Publisher of Junius's Letters are too contemptible to merit the further notice of his pen.

By my own order,
Myself Secretary, POETICASTOS.

LETTER

LETTER XIX.

TO HIS GRACE THE DUKE OF GRAFTON.

MY LORD,   24 *April*, 1769.

THE fyftem you feem to have adopted, when Lord Chatham unexpectedly left you at the head of affairs, gave us no promife of that uncommon exertion of vigour, which has fince illuftrated your character, and diftinguifhed your adminiftration. Far from difcovering a fpirit bold enough to invade the firft rights of the people, and the firft principles of the conftitution, you were fcrupulous of exercifing even thofe powers, with which the executive branch of the legiflature is legally invefted. We have not yet forgotten how long Mr. Wilkes was fuffered to appear at large, nor how long he was at liberty to canvafs for the city and county, with all the terrors of an outlawry hanging over him. Our gracious Sovereign has not yet forgotten the extraordinary care you took of his dignity and of the fafety of his perfon, when at a crifis which courtiers affected to call alarming, you left the metropolis expofed, for two nights together, to every fpecies of riot and diforder. The fecurity of the Royal refidence from infult insult was then sufficiently provided for in Mr. Conway's firmness, and Lord Weymouth's discretion; while the prime minister of Great Britain, in a rural retirement, and in the arms of faded beauty, had lost all memory of his Sovereign, his country and himself. In these instances you might have acted with vigour, for you would have had the sanction of the laws to support you. The friends of government might have defended you without shame, and moderate men, who wish well to the peace and good order of society, might have had a pretence for applauding your conduct. But these it seems were not occasions worthy of your Grace's interposition. You reserved the proofs of your intrepid spirit for trials of greater hazard and importance; and now, as if the most disgraceful relaxation of the executive authority had given you a claim of credit to indulge in excesses still more dangerous, you seem determined to compensate amply for your former negligence; and to balance the non-execution of the laws with a breach of the constitution. From one extreme you suddenly start to the other, without leaving, between the weakness and the fury of the passions, one moment's interval for the firmness of the understanding.

THESE

THESE observations, general as they are, might easily be extended into a faithful history of your Grace's administration, and perhaps may be the employment of a future hour. But the business of the present moment will not suffer me to look back to a series of events, which cease to be interesting or important, because they are succeeded by a measure so singularly daring, that it excites all our attention, and engrosses all our resentment.

YOUR patronage of Mr. Luttrell has been crowned with success. With this precedent before you, with the principles on which it was established, and with a future house of commons, perhaps less virtuous than the present, every county in England, under the auspices of the Treasury, may be represented as completely as the county of Middlesex. Posterity will be indebted to your Grace for not contenting yourself with a temporary expedient, but entailing upon them the immediate blessings of your administration. Boroughs were already too much at the mercy of government. Counties could neither be purchased nor intimidated. But their solemn determined election may be rejected, and the man they detest may be appointed, by another choice, to represent them in parliament. Yet it is admitted, that the sheriffs obeyed the laws

and

and performed their duty*. The return they made muft have been legal and valid, or undoubtedly they would have been cenfured for making it. With every good-natured allowance for your Grace's youth and inexperience, there are fome things which you cannot but know. You cannot but know that the right of the freeholders to adhere to their choice (even fuppofing it improperly exerted) was as clear and indifputable as that of the houfe of commons to exclude one of their own members?—nor is it poffible for you not to fee the wide diftance there is between the negative power of rejecting one man, and the pofitive power of appointing another. The right of expulfion, in the moft favourable fenfe, is no more than the cuftom of parliament. The right of election is the very effence of the conftitution. To violate that right, and much more to transfer it to any other fet of men, is a ftep leading immediately to the diffolution of all government. So far forth as it operates, it conftitutes a houfe of commons, which *does not* reprefent the people. A houfe of commons fo formed would involve a contradiction and the groffeft confufion of ideas; but there are fome minifters, my Lord,

* Even Sir Fletcher Norton declared in the houfe of Commons, that the Sheriffs in returning Mr. Wilkes, had done no more than their duty.

whofe

whose views can only be answered by reconciling absurdities, and making the same proposition, which is false and absurd in argument, true in fact.

'This measure, my Lord, is however attended with one consequence, favourable to the people, which I am persuaded you did not foresee. While the contest lay between the ministry and Mr. Wilkes, his situation and private character gave you advantages over him, which common candour, if not the memory of your former friendship, should have forbidden you to make use of. To religious men, you had an opportunity of exaggerating the irregularities of his past life—to moderate men you held forth the pernicious consequences of faction. Men, who with this character, looked no farther than to the object before them, were not dissatisfied at seeing Mr. Wilkes excluded from parliament. You have now taken care to shift the question; or, rather, you have created a new one, in which Mr. Wilkes is no more concerned than any other English gentleman. You have united this country against you on one grand constitutional point, on the decision of which our existence, as a free people, absolutely depends. You have asserted, not in words but in fact, that the representation in parliament does not depend upon the choice of the freeholders.

If

If such a case can possibly happen once, it may happen frequently; it may happen always:—and if three hundred votes, by any mode of reasoning whatsoever, can prevail against twelve hundred, the same reasoning would equally have given Mr. Luttrell his seat with ten votes, or even with one. The consequences of this attack upon the constitution are too plain and palpable not to alarm the dullest apprehension. I trust you will find, that the people of England are neither deficient in spirit nor understanding, though you have treated them, as if they had neither sense to feel, nor spirit to resent. We have reason to thank God and our ancestors, that there never yet was a minister in this country, who could stand the issue of such a conflict; and with every prejudice in favour of your intentions, I see no such abilities in your Grace, as should entitle you to succeed in an enterprize, in which the ablest and basest of your predecessors have found their destruction. You may continue to deceive your gracious master with false representations of the temper and condition of his subjects. You may command a venal vote, because it is the common established appendage of your office. But never hope that the freeholders will make a tame surrender of their rights, or that an English army will join with you in overturning the liberties of their country.

They

They know that their first duty as citizens is paramount to all subsequent engagements, nor will they prefer the discipline or even the honours of their profession to those sacred original rights, which belonged to them before they were soldiers, and which they claim and possess as the birth-right of Englishmen.

Return, my Lord, before it be too late, to that easy insipid system, which you first set out with. Take back your mistress;*—

the

---

* Ann Parsons. When the Duke obtained a divorce from his Wife, he wrote his Mistress the following letter:

Madam,

ON the final difference I had with my lady, I connected myself with you, as one, I thought, whose personal and mental qualifications were such, as would in a great measure alleviate my domestic misfortunes. My expectations, I must do you the justice to say, were perfectly answered; and it would be perhaps difficult even for ill-nature to point out a single defect in your truth and unwearied assiduity to please me; but as I often told you (particularly at our first interview, that I should have nothing in future to charge myself with) that such a course of life was unseemly both in my moral and political character, and that nothing but the necessity could justify the measure, I am now to tell you (that obstacle being removed by the laws) that all our former ties are, from this day, at an end.

I HAVE

the name of friend may be fatal to her, for it leads to treachery and persecution. Indulge the people. Attend Newmarket. Mr. Luttrell may again vacate his seat; and Mr. Wilkes

I HAVE taken care, my dear friend (for I will now totally throw by the lover) to make that establishment for you, as will make you easy in your circumstances for life, chargeable only with this proviso, that your residence be not in these kingdoms; the rest of Europe lies at your choice; and you have only to send me word on your arrival where you are, and the next post shall carry you your first quarterly payment.

ASSURE yourself, that nothing should induce me to act in this manner, but the determined resolution I have taken, now that it is in my power, of speedily entering into chaster connections; and that I am, and ever shall be, with great esteem and friendship,

Your's, &c.

THE ANSWER.

MY VERY DEAR LORD,

(FOR I will not—indeed I cannot—retaliate your coldness) nothing could have surprised me more than your letter. It is very true you did insinuate on our first connection, that it did not totally agree with your principles and situation, as you was then married. I admitted every force of this reasoning, knowing how, in one of your exalted character, appearances should be supported: but, my Lord, little did I think when that marriage was dissolved, and the odium which attended our connections consequently so, that your affections could so mechanically abate, as in an instant thus to sacrifice

the

Wilkes, if not perfecuted, will foon be forgotten. To be weak and inactive is fafer than to be daring and criminal; and wide is the diftance between a riot of the populace and

the lover to the fordid confiderations of intereft or public opinion.

I CAN readily place your defire of parting with me to the love of variety; but, my Lord, what am I to fay to that part of your letter, wherein you infift (as I fhall forfeit every future claim to your munificence) on my leaving thefe kingdoms? Am I to attribute it to malevolence or ill-nature? No, my Lord, the actual fuffering of this fevere fentence (cruel as it is) fhall not wring from me this confeffion. I will call it the lapfe of the heart, the fault of conftitution, or any other fofter name, that will cover the perfon I hold deareft in the world, from the unnatural (yet too often affociated) titles of Seducer and Perfecutor.

MISTAKE me not, my dear Lord, that I want to plead a remiffion of this fentence from the cruelty of being driven from my native kingdom (though I think this fhould have an effect on your feelings) I urge it on a principle as much more refined as it is diftracting; that of being, for ever, feparated from the Man, not the Lord, of my choice.

THOUGH my pride won't permit me to fue for the recovery of a heart, which, I find, is fo obftinately detached from me; yet, my Lord, fuffer me this poor confolation, to live in the fame kingdom with you.—Give me fome time to mitigate a paffion you firft infpired me with; and though I find I muft bid adieu to the
transports

and a convulsion of the whole kingdom. You may live to make the experiment, but no honest man can wish you should survive it.

JUNIUS.

LETTER XX.

TO HIS GRACE THE DUKE OF GRAFTON.

MY LORD,   30 *May* 1769.

IF the measures in which you have been most successful, had been supported by any tolerable appearance of argument, I should have thought my time not ill employed, in continuing to examine your conduct as a minister, and stating it fairly to the public. But when I see questions of the

transports of love, let me hope for the calmer delights of friendship; and do not, at once, overwhelm me with all the agonies of positive—neglected separation.

You inform me, in the close of your letter, " of your speedily entering into chaster connections."—I am resigned!—And may your future lady love like me, but never meet with such returns!—May every hour of your life be brightened by prosperity; and may the happiness of your domestic character ever keep pace with your public one, prays

The unfortunate, &c.

highest

highest national importance, carried as they have been, and the first principles of the constitution openly violated, without argument or decency, I confess, I give up the cause in despair. The meanest of your predecessors had abilities sufficient to give a colour to their measures. If they invaded the rights of the people, they did not dare to offer a direct insult to their understanding; and, in former times, the most venal parliaments made it a condition, in their bargain with the minister, that he should furnish them with some plausible pretences for selling their country and themselves. You have had the merit of introducing a more compendious system of government and logic. You neither address yourself to the passions, nor to the understanding, but simply to the touch. You apply yourself immediately to the feelings of your friends, who, contrary to the forms of parliament, never enter heartily into a debate, until they have divided.

RELINQUISHING, therefore, all idle views of amendment to your Grace, or of benefit to the public, let me be permitted to consider your character and conduct merely as a subject of curious speculation.——There is something in both, which distinguishes you not only from all other ministers, but all other men. It is not that you do wrong by design,

design, but that you should never do right by mistake. It is not that your indolence and your activity have been equally misapplied, but that the first uniform principle, or, if I may call it the genius of your life, should have carried you through every possible change and contradiction of conduct, without the momentary imputation or colour of a virtue; and that the wildest spirit of inconsistency should never once have betrayed you into a wise or honourable action. This, I own, gives an air of singularity to your fortune, as well as to your disposition. Let us look back together to a scene, in which a mind like yours will find nothing to repent of. Let us try, my Lord, how well you have supported the various relations in which you stood, to your sovereign, your country, your friends, and yourself. Give us, if it be possible, some excuse to posterity, and to ourselves, for submitting to your administration. If not the abilities of a great minister, if not the integrity of a patriot, or the fidelity of a friend, shew us, at least the firmness of a man.—For the sake of your mistress, the lover shall be spared. I will not lead her into public, as you have done, nor will I insult the memory of departed beauty. Her sex, which alone made her amiable in your eyes, makes her respectable in mine.

THE

The character of the reputed ancestors of some men, has made it possible for their descendants to be vicious in the extreme, without being degenerate. Those of your Grace, for instance, left no distressing examples of virtue, even to their legitimate posterity, and you may look back with pleasure to an illustrious pedigree, in which heraldy has not left a single good quality upon record to insult or upbraid you. You have better proofs of your descent, my Lord, than the register of a marriage, or any troublesome inheritance of reputation. There are some hereditary strokes of character, by which a family may be as clearly distinguished as by the blackest features of the human face. Charles the First lived and died a hypocrite. Charles the Second was a hypocrite of another sort, and should have died upon the same scaffold. At the distance of a century, we see their different characters happily revived, and blended in your Grace. Sullen and severe without religion, profligate without gaiety, you live like Charles the Second, without being an amiable companion, and, for aught I know, may die as his father did, without the reputation of a martyr.

You had already taken your degrees with credit in those schools, in which the English nobility are formed to virtue, when you were

were introduced to Lord Chatham's protection. From Newmarket, White's, and the opposition,* he gave you to the world with an air of popularity, which young men usually set out with, and seldom preserve:—grave and plausible enough to be thought fit for business; too young for treachery; and, in short, a patriot of no unpromising expectations. Lord Chatham was the earliest object of your political wonder and attachment; yet you deserted him, upon the first hopes that offered of an equal share of power with Lord Rockingham. When the Duke of Cumberland's first negociation failed, and when the favourite was pushed to the last extremity, you saved him, by joining with an administration, in which Lord Chatham had refused to engage. Still, however, he was your friend, and you are yet to explain to the

* In March 1763, his Grace was in the Opposition to Lord Bute's Administration, and voted against the Cyder Bill. In November the same year he was in the Opposition to the Grenville Administration, and protested against the House voting away privilege in cases of libel. In 1764 he was a Member of the Minority Club at Wildman's Tavern in Albemarle Street: this Club, at its first institution, consisted of 36 Lords and 113 Commoners; in all 149; but it soon dwindled away. In 1765 his Grace came in with the Marquis of Rockingham as a supporter of that nobleman's Administration. See notes to page 5th.

world, why you confented to act without him, or why, after uniting with Lord Rockingham, you deferted and betrayed him. You complained that no meafures were taken to fatisfy your patron, and that your friend, Mr. Wilkes, who had fuffered fo much for the party, had been abandoned to his fate. They have fince contributed not a little, to your prefent plenitude of power; yet, I think, Lord Chatham had lefs reafon than ever to be fatisfied; and as for Mr. Wilkes, it is, perhaps, the greateft misfortune of his life, that you fhould have fo many compenfations to make in the clofet for your former friendfhip with him. Your gracious mafter underftands your character, and makes you a perfecutor, becaufe you have been a friend.

Lord Chatham formed his laft adminiftration upon principles which you certainly concurred in, or you could never have been placed at the head of the treafury. By deferting thofe principles, and by acting in direct contradiction to them, in which he found you were fecretly fupported in the clofet, you foon forced him to leave you to yourfelf, and to withdraw his name from an adminiftration, which had been formed on the credit of it. You had then a profpect of friendfhips better fuited to your genius, and more likely to fix your difpofition. Marriage

riage is the point on which every rake is stationary at last; and truly, my Lord, you may well be weary of the circuit you have taken, for you have now fairly travelled through every sign in the political zodiac, from the Scorpion, in which you stung Lord Chatham, to the hopes of a Virgin * in the House of Bloomsbury. One would think that you had had sufficient experience of the frailty of nuptial engagements, or, at least, that such a friendship as the Duke of Bedford's might have been secured to you by the auspicious marriage of your late Duchess with † his nephew. But ties of this tender nature cannot be drawn too close; and it may possibly be a part of the Duke of Bedford's ambition, after making her an honest woman, to work a miracle of the same sort upon your Grace. This worthy Nobleman has long dealt in virtue. There has been a large consumption of it in his own family; and, in the way of traffic, I dare say, he has bought and sold more than half the representative integrity of the nation.

* His Grace had lately married Miss Wrottesley, niece of the Duchess of Bedford.

† Miss LIDDELL after being divorced from the Duke, married the Earl of Upper Ossory.

'In a political view, this union is not imprudent. The favour of princes is a perishable commodity. You have now a strength sufficient to command the closet; and, if it be necessary to betray one friendship more, you may set even Lord Bute at defiance. Mr. Stuart Mackenzie may possibly remember what use the Duke of Bedford usually makes of his power; and our gracious Sovereign, I doubt not, rejoices at this first appearance of union among his servants. His late Majesty, under the happy influence of a family connection between his ministers, was relieved from the cares of the government. A more active prince may perhaps observe, with suspicion, by what degrees an artful servant grows upon his master, from the first unlimited professions of duty and attachment, to the painful representation of the necessity of the royal service, and soon, in regular progression, to the humble insolence of dictating in all the obsequious forms of peremptory submission. The interval is carefully employed in forming connections, creating interests, collecting a party, and laying the foundation of double marriages; until the deluded prince, who thought he had found a creature prostituted to his service, and insignificant enough to be always dependent upon his pleasure, finds him at last too strong to be commanded, and too formidable to be removed.

Your Grace's public conduct, as a minister, is but the counter part of your private history;—the same inconsistency, the same contradictions. In America we trace you, from the first opposition to the Stamp Act, on principles of convenience, to Mr. Pitt's surrender of the right; then forward to Lord Rockingham's surrender of the fact; then back again to Lord Rockingham's declaration of the right; then forward to taxation with Mr. Townshend; and in the last instance, from the gentle Conway's undetermined discretion, to blood and compulsion with the Duke of Bedford: Yet if we may believe the simplicity of Lord North's eloquence, at the opening of next sessions you are once more to be the patron of America. Is this the wisdom of a great minister? or is it the ominous vibration of a pendulum? Had you no opinion of your own, my Lord? or was it the gratification of betraying every party with which you have been united, and of deserting every political principle, in which you had concurred?

Your enemies may turn their eyes without regret from this admirable system of provincial government. They will find gratification

tion enough in the survey of your domestic and foreign policy.

If, instead of disowning Lord Shelburne, the British court had interposed with dignity and firmness, you know, my Lord, that Corsica would never have been invaded. The French saw the weakness of a distracted ministry, and were justified in treating you with contempt. They would probably have yielded in the first instance, rather than hazard a rupture with this country; but, being once engaged, they cannot retreat without dishonour. Common sense foresees consequences, which have escaped your Grace's penetration. Either we suffer the French to make an acquisition, the importance of which you have probably no conception of, or we oppose them by an underhand management, which only disgraces us in the eyes of Europe, without answering any purpose of policy or prudence. From secret, indirect assistance, a transition to some more open decisive measures becomes unavoidable; till at last we find ourselves principal in the war, and are obliged to hazard every thing for an object, which might have originally been obtained without expence or danger. I am not versed in the politics of the north; but this I believe is certain, that half the money you have distributed to carry the expulsion of

Mr.

Mr. Wilkes, or even your Secretary's share in the last subscription, would have kept the Turks at your devotion. Was it œconomy, my Lord? or did the coy resistance you have constantly met with in the British senate, make you despair of corrupting the Divan? Your friends indeed have the first claim upon your bounty, but if five hundred pounds a year can be spared in a pension to Sir John Moore, it would not have disgraced you to have allowed something to the secret service of the public.

You will say perhaps that the situation of affairs at home demanded and engrossed the whole of your attention. Here, I confess, you have been active. An amiable, accomplished prince ascends the throne under the happiest of all auspices, the acclamations and united affections of his subjects. The first measures of his reign, and even the odium of a favourite, were not able to shake their attachment. Your services, my Lord, have been more successful. Since you were permitted to take the lead, we have seen the natural effects of a system of government, at once both odious and contemptible. We have seen the laws sometimes scandalously relaxed, sometimes violently stretched beyond their tone. We have seen the person of the Sovereign insulted; and in profound peace,
and

and with an undisputed title, the fidelity of his subjects brought by his own servants into public question. Without abilities, resolution, or interest, you have done more than Lord Bute could accomplish with all Scotland at his heels.

Your Grace, little anxious perhaps either for present or future reputation, will not desire to be handed down in these colours to posterity. You have reason to flatter yourself that the memory of your administration will survive even the forms of a constitution, which our ancestors vainly hoped would be immortal; and as for your personal character, I will not, for the honour of human nature, suppose that you can wish to have it remembered. The condition of the present times is desperate indeed; but there is a debt due to those who come after us, and it is the historian's office to punish, though he cannot correct. I do not give you to posterity as a pattern to imitate, but as an example to deter; and as your conduct comprehends every thing that a wise or honest minister should avoid, I mean to make you a negative instruction to your successors for ever.

JUNIUS.

LETTER XXI.

TO THE PRINTER OF THE PUBLIC ADVERTISER.

SIR, 12 *June*, 1769.

THE Duke of Grafton's friends, not finding it convenient to enter into a conteſt with Junius, are now reduced to the laſt melancholy reſource of defeated argument, the flat general charge of ſcurrility and falſehood. As for his ſtile, I ſhall leave it to the critics. The truth of his facts is of more importance to the public. They are of ſuch a nature, that I think a bare contradiction will have no weight with any man, who judges for himſelf. Let us take them in the order in which they appear in his laſt letter.

1. HAVE not the firſt rights of the people, and the firſt principles of the conſtitution been openly invaded, and the very name of an election made ridiculous by the arbitrary appointment of Mr. Luttrell?

2. DID not the Duke of Grafton frequently lead his miſtreſs into public, and even place

place her at the head of his table, as if he had pulled down an ancient temple of Venus, and could bury all decency and shame under the ruins?—Is this the man who dares to talk of Mr. Wilkes's morals?

3. Is not the character of his presumptive ancestors as strongly marked in him, as if he had descended from them in a direct legitimate line? The idea of his death is only prophetic; and what is prophecy but a narrative preceding the fact?

4. Was not Lord Chatham the first who raised him to the rank and post of a minister, and the first whom he abandoned?

5. Did he not join with Lord Rockingham, and betray him?

6. Was he not the bosom friend of Mr. Wilkes, whom he now pursues to destruction?

7. Did he not take his degrees with credit at Newmarket, White's, and the opposition?

8. After deserting Lord Chatham's principles, and sacrificing his friendship, is he not now closely united with a set of men, who, tho' they have occasionally joined with all parties, have

have in every different situation, and at all times, been equally and constantly detested by this country?

9. Has not Sir John Moore a pension of five hundred pounds a year?—This may probably be an acquittance of favours upon the turf; but is it possible for a minister to offer a grosser outrage to a nation, which has so very lately cleared away the beggary of the civil list, at the expence of more than half a million?

10. Is there any one mode of thinking or acting with respect to America, which the Duke of Grafton has not successively adopted and abandoned?

11. Is there not a singular mark of shame set upon this man, who has so little delicacy and feeling as to submit to the opprobrium of marrying a near relation of one who had debauched his wife?—In the name of decency, how are these amiable cousins to meet at their uncle's table?—It will be a scene in Œdipus, without the distress.—Is it wealth, or wit, or beauty,—or is the amorous youth in love?

THE rest is notorious. That Corsica has been sacrificed to the French: that in some instances the laws have been scandalously relaxed,

laxed, and in others daringly violated; and that the king's subjects have been called upon to assure him of their fidelity, in spite of the measures of his servants.

A WRITER who builds his arguments upon facts such as these, is not easily to be confuted. He is not to be answered by general assertions, or general reproaches. He may want eloquence to amuse and persuade, but, speaking truth, he must always convince.

PHILO JUNIUS.

LETTER XXII.

REPLY TO LETTER XX. SIGNED JUNIUS.

THE author of the letter signed Junius has comprehended all the charges that a disappointed faction, or the malice of his inveterate enemies could invent, against the private character and family of the Duke of Grafton.

THOSE charges I will answer briefly, and for ever after drop the subject.

1. THE rights of the people were so far from being invaded in the affair of the elec-

tion for the county of Middlesex, that not only two thirds of the nation have in the most public and solemn manner approved of that measure, but also the most eminent lawyers in England, with the Chancellor at their head, declared that the accepting of Mr. Luttrell for member was perfectly legal and constitutional.

2. WHETHER the Duke of Grafton led his mistress into public is a fact to which I am an utter stranger; and if he had, there is scarcely a gentleman in England but has been at one time or other, seen at a public place with his female friend.

3. EVERY dispassionate man in the kingdom must own that the weaknesses of the unhappy family, who lost by their folly the crown of Great Britain, have been too much exaggerated, and that their crimes proceeded more from error in judgment, than from any malignity of mind. They were certainly more unfortunate than criminal.

4. LORD CHATHAM, it is true, was the capital figure in the administration in 1766; but so far was the Duke of Grafton from deserting him, that of his own accord in 1768, he begged that his name might be taken from councils, at which the weak state of his body

body and mind made him incapable to assist.

5. THE Duke of Grafton during the course of Lord Rockingham's administration, saw that the Marquis was altogether unfit for public business. He did not desert the Marquis, but the Marquis deserted those firm principles upon which the Duke wished to carry on the business of the nation.

6. IF the Duke of Grafton was ever acquainted with Mr. Wilkes, it was at a time when the infamy of his character was unknown to the world. To desert the acquaintance of a man destitute of virtue is real praise: neither can enforcing the law against the vicious be called persecution.

7. THE Duke of Grafton was admitted to Newmarket, White's, and opposition; so have almost all the men of family and fashion in the nation.

8. THAT the Duke of Bedford has ever been detested by his country, is an absolute falsehood; some of his followers have, indeed, been covered with abuse; but their abilities are universally allowed, and their honour and patriotism remain unimpeached.

9. THE

9. The penſion given to Sir John Moore, does honour to the humanity of the Duke of Grafton, if Sir John has been unfortunate becauſe honeſt, it is an act worthy of praiſe to ſupport a numerous family, involved in diſtreſs more by the misfortunes, than by the crimes of their parents.

10. Ill underſtood, and deſignedly involved in obſcurity, the affairs of America bore, at different times, different aſpects. The Duke of Grafton has been invariably fixed to ſtrike the happy medium between the intereſts of America, and the preſervation of the authority of the mother country. If, in the courſe of this deſign, he has changed his meaſures, we are to attribute this to his prudence, and not to the verſatility of his mind.

The laſt article deſerves no anſwer: the factious diſpoſition of the writer has defeated the deſigned effect of his abuſe. In one part of his letter he blames his Grace for keeping a miſtreſs,—in another for taking a lawful wife. The truth is, faction is determined not to be pleaſed. They want to poſſeſs themſelves of the treaſury, and until the Duke reſigns that ſweet morſel to the devouring jaws of oppoſition, it will for ever ſpit forth venom and defamation. But the Duke of Grafton deſpiſes ill founded abuſe, as much

much as he abhors the commission of the crime falsely laid to his charge.

OLD NOLL.

LETTER XXIII.

TO THE PRINTER OF THE PUBLIC
ADVERTISER.

SIR, 22. *June*, 1769.

THE name of Old Noll is destined to be the ruin of the house of Stuart. There is an ominous fatality in it, which even the spurious descendants of the family cannot escape. Oliver Cromwell had the merit of conducting Charles the first to the block. Your correspondent Old Noll appears to have the same design upon the Duke of Grafton. His arguments consist better with the title he has assumed, than with the principles he professes; for though he pretends to be an advocate for the Duke, he takes care to give us the best reasons, why his patron should regularly follow the fate of his presumptive ancestor.—Through the whole course of the Duke of Grafton's life, I see a strange endeavour to unite contradictions, which cannot be reconciled. He marries to be divorced:—He keeps a mistress to remind him of conjugal endearments, and he chooses such friends, as it is virtue in him to desert. If it were possible for the genius of that accomplished president, who pronounced sentence upon Charles the first, to be revived in some modern sycophant *, his Grace I doubt not would by sympathy discover him among the dregs of mankind, and take him for a guide in those paths, which naturally conduct a minister to the scaffold.

THE assertion that two-thirds of the nation approve of the acceptance of Mr. Luttrell (for even Old Noll is too modest to call it an election) can neither be maintained nor confuted by argument. It is a point of fact, on which every English gentleman will determine for himself. As to lawyers, their profession is supported by the indiscriminate defence of right and wrong, and I confess I have not that opinion of their knowledge or integrity, to think it necessary that they should decide for me upon a plain constitutional question. With respect to the appointment of Mr. Luttrell, the chancellor has never yet given any authentic opinion. Sir Fletcher Norton is indeed an honest, a very honest man; and the Attorney General is *ex officio* the guardian

---

* Mr. Bradshaw, then secretary to the Treasury.

of liberty, to take care, I presume, that it shall never break out into a criminal excess. Doctor Blackstone is Solicitor to the Queen. The Doctor recollected that he had a place to preserve, though he forgot that he had a reputation to lose. We have now the good fortune to understand the Doctor's principles, as well as writings. For the defence of truth, of law, and reason, the Doctor's book may be safely consulted; but whoever wishes to cheat a neighbour of his estate, or to rob a country of its rights, need make no scruple of consulting the Doctor himself.

THE example of the English nobility may, for aught I know, sufficiently justify the Duke of Grafton, when he indulges his genius in all the fashionable excesses of the age; yet, considering his rank and station, I think it would do him more honour to be able to deny the fact, than to defend it by such authority. But if vice itself could be excused, there is yet a certain display of it, a certain outrage to decency, and violation of public decorum, which, for the benefit of society, should never be forgiven. It is not that he kept a mistress at home, but that he constantly attended her abroad.—It is not the private indulgence, but the public insult of which I complain. The name of Miss Parsons would hardly have been known, if

the

the First Lord of the Treasury had not led her in triumph through the Opera House, even in the presence of the Queen. When we see a man act in this manner, we may admit the shameless depravity of his heart, but what are we to think of his understanding.

His Grace it seems is now to be a regular domestic man, and as an omen of the future delicacy and correctness of his conduct, he marries a first cousin of the man, who had fixed that mark and title of infamy upon him, which, at the same moment, makes a husband unhappy and ridiculous. The ties of consanguinity may possibly preserve him from the same fate a second time, and as to the distress of meeting, I take it for granted the venerable uncle of these common cousins has settled the etiquette in such a manner, that, if a mistake should happen, it may reach no farther than from Madame ma femme to Madame ma cousine.

The Duke of Grafton has always some excellent reason for deserting his friends.—The age and incapacity of Lord Chatham;—the debility of Lord Rockingham;—or the infamy of Mr. Wilkes. There was a time indeed when he did not appear to be quite so well acquainted, or so violently offended with the infirmities of his friends. But now I confess fefs they are not ill exchanged for the youthful, vigorous virtue of the Duke of Bedford;—the firmnefs of General Conway;— the blunt, or if I may call it, the aukward integrity of Mr. Rigby, and the fpotlefs morality of Lord Sandwich.

IF a late penfion to a * broken gambler be an act worthy of commendation, the Duke of Grafton's connexions will furnifh him with many opportunities of doing praife-worthy actions; and as he himfelf bears no part of the expence, the generofity of diftributing the public money for the fupport of virtuous families in diftrefs will be an unqueftionable proof of his Grace's humanity.

As to public affairs, Old Noll is a little tender of defcending to particulars. He does not deny that Corfica has been facrificed to France, and he confeffes that, with regard to America, his patron's meafures have been fubject to fome variation; but then he promifes wonders of ftability and firmnefs for the future. Thefe are myfteries, of which we muft not pretend to judge by experience; and truly, I fear we fhall perifh in the Defart, before we arrive at the Land of Promife. In the regular courfe of things, the period of

* Sir John Moore.

the

the Duke of Grafton's minifterial manhood fhould now be approaching. The imbecility of his infant ftate was committed to Lord Chatham. Charles Townfhend took fome care of his education at that ambiguous age, which lies between the follies of political childhood, and the vices of puberty. The empire of the paffions foon fucceeded. His earlieft principles and connexions were of courfe forgotten, or defpifed. The company he has lately kept has been of no fervice to his morals; and, in the conduct of public affairs, we fee the character of his time of life ftrongly diftinguifhed. An obftinate ungovernable felf-fufficiency plainly points out to us that ftate of imperfect maturity, at which the graceful levity of youth is loft, and the folidity of experience not yet acquired. It is poffible the young man may in time grow wifer and reform; but, if I underftand his difpofition, it is not of fuch corrigible ftuff, that we fhould hope for any amendment in him; before he has accomplifhed the deftruction of this country. Like other rakes, he may perhaps live to fee his error, but not untill he has ruined his eftate.

PHILO JUNIUS.

LETTER

LETTER XXIV.

TO HIS GRACE THE DUKE OF GRAFTON.

MY LORD, 8 *July*, 1769.

IF nature had given you an understanding qualified to keep pace with the wishes and principles of your heart, she would have made you, perhaps, the most formidable minister that ever was employed, under a limited monarch, to accomplish the ruin of a free people. When neither the feelings of shame, the reproaches of conscience, nor the dread of punishment, form any bar to the designs of a minister, the people would have too much reason to lament their condition, if they did not find some resource in the weakness of his understanding. We owe it to the bounty of providence, that the completest depravity of the heart is sometimes strangely united with a confusion of the mind, which counteracts the most favourite principles, and makes the same man treacherous without art, and a hypocrite without deceiving. The measures, for instance, in which your Grace's activity has been chiefly exerted, as they were adopted without skill, should have been conducted with more than common dexterity.
But

But truly, my Lord, the execution has been as gross as the design. By one decisive step, you have defeated all the arts of writing. You have fairly confounded the intrigues of opposition, and silenced the clamours of faction. A dark, ambiguous system might require and furnish the materials of ingenius illustration; and, in doubtful measures, the virulent exaggeration of party must be employed, to rouse and engage the passions of the people. You have now brought the merits of your administration to an issue, on which every Englishman of the narrowest capacity may determine for himself. It is not an alarm to the passions, but a calm appeal to the judgement of the people, upon their own most essential interests. A more experienced minister would not have hazarded a direct invasion of the first principles of the constitution, before he had made some progress in subduing the spirit of the people. With such a cause as yours, my Lord, it is not sufficient that you have the court at your devotion, unless you can find means to corrupt or intimidate the jury. The collective body of the people form that jury, and from their decision there is but one appeal.

WHETHER you have talents to support you, at a crisis of such difficulty and danger, should long since have been considered. Judging

ing truly of your difposition, you have perhaps miftaken the extent of your capacity. Good faith and folly have fo long been received as fynonimous terms, that the reverfe of the propofition has grown into credit, and every villain fancies himfelf a man of abilities. It is the apprehenfion of your friends, my Lord, that you have drawn fome hafty conclufion of this fort, and that a partial reliance upon your moral character has betrayed you beyond the depth of your underftanding. You have now carried things too far to retreat. You have plainly declared to the people what they are to expect from the continuance of your adminiftration. It is time for your Grace to confider what you alfo may expect in return from their fpirit and their refentment.

SINCE the acceffion of our moft gracious Sovereign to the throne, we have feen a fyftem of government, which may well be called a reign of experiments. Parties of all denominations have been employed and difmiffed. The advice of the ableft men in this country has been repeatedly called for and rejected; and when the Royal difpleafure has been fignified to a minifter, the marks of it have ufually been proportioned to his abilities and integrity. The fpirit of the Favourite had fome apparent influence upon every adminiftration; and every fet of minifters preferved

an

an appearance of duration, as long as they submitted to that influence. But there were certain services to be performed for the Favourite's security, or to gratify his resentments, which your predecessors in office had the wisdom or the virtue not to undertake. The moment this refractory spirit was discovered, their disgrace was determined. Lord Chatham, Mr. Grenville, and Lord Rockingham have successively had the honour to be dismissed for preferring their duty, as servants of the public, to those compliances which were expected from their station. A submissive administration was at last gradually collected from the deserters of all parties, interests, and connexions: and nothing remained but to find a leader for these gallant well-disciplined troops. Stand forth, my Lord, for thou art the man. Lord Bute found no resource of dependence or security in the proud, imposing superiority of Lord Chatham's abilities, the shrewd inflexible judgement of Mr. Grenville, nor in the mild but determined integrity of Lord Rockingham. His views and situation required a creature void of all these properties; and he was forced to go through every division, resolution, composition, and refinement of political chemistry, before he happily arrived at the caput mortuum of vitriol in your Grace. Flat and insipid in your retired state, but brought into action

action you become vitriol again. Such are
the extremes of alternate indolence or fury,
which have governed your whole administration. Your circumstances with regard
to the people soon becoming desperate, like
other honest servants, you determined to involve the best of masters in the same difficulties with yourself. We owe it to your
Grace's well-directed labours, that your Sovereign has been persuaded to doubt of the
affections of his subjects, and the people to
suspect the virtues of their Sovereign, at a
time when both were unquestionable. You
have degraded the Royal dignity into a base,
dishonourable competition with Mr. Wilkes,
nor had you abilities to carry even the last
contemptible triumph over a private man,
without the grossest violation of the fundamental laws of the constitution and rights of
the people. But these are rights, my Lord,
which you can no more annihilate, than you
can the soil to which they are annexed. The
question no longer turns upon points of national honour and security abroad, or on the
degrees of expedience and propriety of measures at home. It was not inconsistent that
you should abandon the cause of liberty in
another country, which you had persecuted
in your own; and in the common arts of
domestic corruption, we miss no part of Sir
Robert Walpole's system, except his abilities.

Vol. I. · G In

In this humble imitative line, you might long have proceeded, safe and contemptible. You might probably never have risen to the dignity of being hated, and even have been despised with moderation. But it seems you meant to be distinguished, and, to a mind like yours, there was no other road to fame but by the destruction of a noble fabric, which you thought had been too long the admiration of mankind. The use you have made of the military force introduced an alarming change in the mode of executing the laws. The arbitrary appointment of Mr. Luttrell invades the foundation of the laws themselves, as it manifestly transfers the right of legislation from those whom the people have chosen, to those whom they have rejected. With a succession of such appointments, we may soon see a house of commons collected, in the choice of which the other towns and counties of England will have as little share as the devoted county of Middlesex.

YET I trust your Grace will find that the people of this country are neither to be intimidated by violent measures, nor deceived by refinements. When they see Mr. Luttrell seated in the house of commons by mere dint of power, and in direct opposition to the choice of a whole county, they will not listen to those subtleties, by which

which every arbitrary exertion of authority is explained into the law and privilege of parliament. It requires no perfuasion of argument, but fimply the evidence of the fenfes, to convince them, that to transfer the right of election from the collective to the reprefentative body of the people, contradicts all thofe ideas of a houfe of commons, which they have received from their forefathers, and which they had already, though vainly perhaps, delivered to their children. The principles, on which this violent meafure has been defended, have added fcorn to injury, and forced us to feel, that we are not only oppreffed but infulted.

WITH what force, my Lord, with what protection, are you prepared to meet the united deteftation of the people of England? The city of London has given a generous example to the kingdom, in what manner a king of this country ought to be addreffed; and I fancy, my Lord, it is not yet in your courage to ftand between your Sovereign and the addreffes of his fubjects, The injuries you have done this country are fuch as demand not only redrefs, but vengeance. In vain fhall you look for protection to that venal vote, which you have already paid for —another muft be purchafed; and to fave a minifter, the houfe of commons muft declare themselves not only independent of their constituents, but the determined enemies of the constitution. Consider, my Lord, whether this be an extremity to which their fears will permit them to advance; or, if their protection should fail you, how far you are authorised to rely upon the sincerity of those smiles, which a pious court lavishes without reluctance upon a libertine by profession. It is not indeed the least of the thousand contradictions which attend you, that a man, marked to the world by the grossest violation of all ceremony and decorum, should be the first servant of a court, in which prayers are morality, and kneeling is religion. Trust not too far to appearances, by which your predecessors have been deceived, though they have not been injured. Even the best of princes may at last discover, that this is a contention, in which every thing may be lost, but nothing can be gained; and as you became minister by accident, were adopted without choice, trusted without confidence, and continued without favour, be assured that, whenever an occasion presses, you will be discarded without even the forms of regret. You will then have reason to be thankful, if you are permitted to retire to that seat of learning, which, in contemplation of the system of your life, the comparative purity of your manners with those of their high steward,

ard, and a thousand other recommending circumstances, has chosen you to encourage the growing virtue of their youth, and to preside over their education. Whenever the spirit of distributing prebends and bishopricks shall have departed from you, you will find that learned seminary perfectly recovered from the delirium of an installation, and, what in truth it ought to be, once more a peaceful scene of slumber and thoughtless meditation. The venerable tutors of the university will no longer distress your modesty, by proposing you for a pattern to their pupils. The learned dulness of declamation will be silent; and even the venal muse, though happiest in fiction, will forget your virtues. Yet, for the benefit of the succeeding age, I could wish that your retreat might be deferred, until your morals shall happily be ripened to that maturity of corruption, at which the worst examples cease to be contagious.

LETTER XXV.

TO THE PRINTER OF THE PUBLIC ADVERTISER.

SIR, 19 *July*, 1769.

A GREAT deal of useless argument might have been saved, in the political contest, which has arisen from the expulsion of Mr. Wilkes, and the subsequent appointment of Mr. Luttrell, if the question had been once stated with precision, to the satisfaction of each party, and clearly understood by them both. But in this, as in almost every other dispute, it usually happens that much time is lost in referring to a multitude of cases and precedents, which prove nothing to the purpose, or in maintaining propositions, which are either not disputed, or, whether they be admitted or denied, are entirely indifferent as to the matter in debate; until at last the mind, perplexed and confounded with the endless subtleties of controversy, loses sight of the main question, and never arrives at truth. Both parties in the dispute are apt enough to practise these dishonest artifices. The man, who is conscious of the weakness of his cause, is interested in concealing it: and, on the other
side,

side, it is not uncommon to see a good cause mangled by advocates, who do not know the real strength of it.

I should be glad to know, for instance, to what purpose, in the present case, so many precedents have been produced to prove, that the house of commons have a right to expel one of their own members; that it belongs to them to judge of the validity of elections; or that the law of parliament is part of the law of the land? After all these propositions are admitted, * Mr. Luttrell's right to his seat will continue to be just as disputable as it was before. Not one of them is at present in agitation. Let it be admitted that the house of commons were authorised to expel Mr. Wilkes; that they are the proper court to judge of elections, and that the law of parliament is binding upon the people; still it remains to be enquired whether the house, by their resolution in favour of Mr. Luttrell, have or have not truly declared that law. To facilitate this enquiry, I would have the question cleared of all foreign or indifferent matter. The following state of it will probably be thought a fair one by both parties; and then I imagine there is no

* They are only admitted, for the sake of argument, and to bring the question to issue.

gentle-

gentleman in this country, who will not be capable of forming a judicious and true opinion upon it. I take the question to be strictly this: " Whether or no it be the "known, established law of parliament, that "the expulsion of a member of the house "of commons of itself creates in him such "an incapacity to be re-elected, that, at a "subsequent election, any votes given to "him are null and void, and that any other "candidate, who, except the person expel- "led, has the greatest number of votes, ought "to be the sitting member."

To prove that the affirmative is the law of parliament, I apprehend it is not sufficient for the present house of commons to declare it to be so. We may shut our eyes indeed to the dangerous consequences of suffering one branch of the legislature to declare new laws, without argument or example, and it may perhaps be prudent enough to submit to authority; but a mere assertion will never convince, much less it will be thought reasonable to prove the right by the fact itself. The ministry have not yet pretended to such a tyranny over our minds. To support the affirmative fairly, it will either be necessary to produce some statute, in which that positive provision shall have been made, that specific disability clearly created, and the consequences

sequences of it declared; or, if there be no such statute, the custom of parliament must then be referred to, and some case or cases*, strictly in point, must be produced, with the decision of the court upon them: for I readily admit that the custom of parliament, once clearly proved, is equally binding with the common and statute law.

The consideration of what may be reasonable or unreasonable makes no part of this question. We are enquiring what the law is, not what it ought to be. Reason may be applied to shew the impropriety or expedience of a law, but we must have either statute or precedent to prove the existence of it. At the same time I do not mean to admit that the late resolution of the house of commons is defensible on general principles of reason, any more than in law. This is not the hinge on which the debate turns.

Supposing therefore that I have laid down an accurate state of the question, I will venture to affirm, 1st, That there is no statute existing by which that specific disability which we speak of is created. If there be,

---

* Junius thought it necessary to meet ministry on their own ground; though precedents in opposition to principles, have little weight with him.

let it be produced. The argument will then be at an end.

2dly, THAT there is no precedent in all the proceedings of the houſe of commons which comes entirely home to the preſent caſe, viz. " where an expelled member has " been returned again, and another candi- " date, with an inferior number of votes, " has been declared the ſitting member." If there be ſuch a precedent, let it be given to us plainly, and I am ſure it will have more weight than all the cunning arguments which have been drawn from inferences and probabilities.

THE miniſtry, in that laborious pamphlet which I preſume contains the whole ſtrength of the party, have declared*, " That Mr. " Walpole's was the firſt and only inſtance, " in which the electors of any county or bo- " rough had returned a perſon expelled to " ſerve in the ſame parliament." It is not poſſible to conceive a caſe more exactly in point. Mr. Walpole was expelled, and, having a majority of votes at the next election, was returned again. The friends of Mr. Taylor, a candidate ſet up by the miniſtry, petitioned the houſe that he might

* *Caſe of the Middleſex election conſidered*, page 38.

be

be the sitting member. Thus far the circumstances tally exactly, except that our house of commons saved Mr. Luttrell the trouble of petitioning. The point of law however was the same. It came regularly before the house, and it was their business to determine upon it. They did determine it, for they declared Mr. Taylor *not duly elected*. If it be said that they meant this resolution as matter of favour and indulgence to the borough, which had retorted Mr. Walpole upon them, in order that the burgesses, knowing what the law was, might correct their error. I answer,

I. THAT it is a strange way of arguing to oppose a supposition, which no man can prove, to a fact which proves itself.

II. THAT if this were the intention of the house of commons, it must have defeated itself. The burgesses of Lynn could never have known their error, much less could they have corrected it by any instruction they received from the proceedings of the house of commons. They might perhaps have foreseen, that, if they returned Mr. Walpole again, he would again be rejected; but they never could infer, from a resolution by which the candidate with the fewest votes was declared *not duly elected*, that, at a future election

tion, and in similar circumstances, the house of commons would reverse their resolution, and receive the same candidate as duly elected, whom they had before rejected.

This indeed would have been a most extraordinary way of declaring the law of parliament, and what I presume no man, whose understanding is not at cross purposes with itself, could possibly understand.

If, in a case of this importance, I thought myself at liberty to argue from suppositions rather than from facts, I think the probability, in this instance, is directly the reverse of what the ministry affirm; and that it is much more likely that the house of commons at that time would rather have strained a point in favour of Mr. Taylor, than that they would have violated the law of parliament, and robbed Mr. Taylor of a right legally vested in him, to gratify a refractory borough, which in defiance of them, had returned a person branded with the strongest mark of the displeasure of the house.

But really, Sir, this way of talking, for I cannot call it argument, is a mockery of the common understanding of the nation, too gross to be endured. Our dearest interests are at stake. An attempt has been made, not

merely

merely to rob a single county of its rights, but, by inevitable consequence, to alter the constitution of the house of commons. This fatal attempt has succeeded, and stands as a precedent recorded for ever. If the ministry are unable to defend their cause by fair argument founded on facts, let them spare us at least the mortification of being amused and deluded like children. I believe there is yet a spirit of resistance in this country, which will not submit to be oppressed; but I am sure there is a fund of good sense in this country, which cannot be deceived.

JUNIUS.

LETTER XXVI.

TO THE PRINTER OF THE PUBLIC ADVERTISER.

S I R,   1 *August*, 1769.

IT will not be necessary for *Junius* to take the trouble of answering your correspondent G. A. or the quotation from a speech without doors, published in your paper of the 28th of last month. The speech appeared before *Junius*'s letter, and as the author seems to consider the great proposition, on which all his argument depends, viz. *that Mr. Wilkes*
was

was under that known legal incapacity, of which Junius speaks, as a point granted, his speech is, in no shape, an answer to *Junius,* for this is the very question in debate.

As to G. A. I observe first, that if he did not admit *Junius*'s state of the question, he should have shewn the fallacy of it, or given us a more exact one;—secondly, that, considering the many hours and days, which the ministry and their advocates have wasted, in public debate, in compiling large quartos, and collecting innumerable precedents, expressly to prove that the late proceedings of the house of commons are warranted by the law, custom, and practice of parliament, it is rather an extraordinary supposition, to be made by one of their own party even for the sake of argument, *that no such statute, no such custom of parliament, no such case in point can be produced.* G. A. may however make the supposition with safety. It contains nothing, but literally the fact, except that there is a case exactly in point, with a decision of the house diametrically opposite to that which the present house of commons came to in favour of Mr. Luttrell.

The ministry now begin to be ashamed of the weakness of their cause, and, as it usually happens with falsehood, are driven to the necessity

cessity of shifting their ground, and changing their whole defence. At first we were told that nothing could be clearer than that the proceedings of the house of commons were justified by the known law and uniform custom of parliament. But now it seems, if there be no law, the house of commons have a right to make one, and if there be no precedent, they have a right to create the first;—for this I presume is the amount of the questions proposed to *Junius*. If your correspondent had been at all versed in the law of parliament, or generally in the laws of this country, he would have seen that this defence is as weak and false as the former.

THE privileges of either house of parliament, it is true, are indefinite, that is, they have not been described or laid down in any one code or declaration whatsoever; but whenever a question of privilege has arisen, it has invariably been disputed or maintained upon the footing of precedents alone*. In the course of the proceedings upon the Aylesbury election, the house of lords resolved, " That neither house of parliament had any " power, by any vote or declaration, to

---

* This is again meeting ministry upon their own ground; but precedents cannot vindicate either natural injustice, or violation of positive right.

" create,

"create to themselves any new privilege that was not warranted by the known laws and customs of parliament." And to this rule the house of commons, though otherwise they had acted in a very arbitrary manner, gave their assent, for they affirmed that they had guided themselves by it, in asserting their privileges.—Now, Sir, if this be true with respect to matters of privilege, in which the house of commons, individually and as a body, are principally concerned, how much more strongly will it hold against any pretended power in that house, to create or declare a new law, by which not only the rights of the house over their own member, and those of the member himself are included, but also those of a third and separate party, I mean the freeholders of the kingdom. To do justice to the ministry, they have not yet pretended that any one or any two of the three estates have power to make a new law, without the concurrence of the third. They know that a man who maintains such a doctrine is liable, by statute, to the heaviest penalties. They do not acknowledge that the house of commons have assumed a *new* privilege, or declared a *new* law. On the contrary, they affirm that their proceedings have been strictly conformable to, and founded upon, the ancient law and custom of parliament. Thus therefore the question

question returns to the point, at which *Junius* had fixed it, viz. *Whether or no this be the law of parliament.* If it be not, the house of commons had no legal authority to establish the precedent; and the precedent itself is a mere fact, without any proof of right whatsoever.

Your correspondent concludes with a question of the simplest nature: *Must a thing be wrong, because it has never been done before?* No. But admitting it were proper to be done, that alone does not convey an authority to do it. As to the present case, I hope I shall never see the time, when not only a single person, but a whole county, and in effect the entire collective body of the people, may again be robbed of their birthright by a vote of the house of commons. But if, for reasons which I am unable to comprehend, it be necessary to trust that house with a power so exorbitant and so unconstitutional, at least let it be given to them by an act of the legislature.

PHILO JUNIUS.

LETTER

LETTER XXVII.

TO SIR WILLIAM BLACKSTONE SOLICITOR GENERAL TO HER MAJESTY.

SIR,   29 *July*, 1769.

I SHALL make you no apology for confidering a certain pamphlet*, in which your late conduct is defended, as written by yourfelf, the perfonal interefts, the perfonal refentments, and above all, that wounded fpirit, unaccuftomed to reproach, and I hope not frequently confcious of deferving it, are fignals which betray the author to us as plainly as if your name were in the title-page. You appeal to the public in defence of your reputation. We hold it, Sir, that an injury offered to an individual is interefting to fociety. On this principle the people of England made common caufe with Mr. Wilkes. On this principle, if *you* are injured, they will join in your refentment. I fhall not follow you through the infipid form of a third perfon, but addrefs myfelf to you directly.

* A LETTER to the Author of the Queftion Stated.

You seem to think the channel of a pamphlet more respectable and better suited to the dignity of your cause, than that of a newspaper. Be it so. Yet if newspapers are scurrilous, you must confess they are impartial. They give us, without any apparent preference, the wit and argument of the ministry, as well as the abusive dulness of the opposition. The scales are equally poised. It it not the printer's fault if the greater weight inclines the balance.

Your pamphlet then is divided into an attack upon Mr. Grenville's character, and a defence of your own. It would have been more consistent perhaps with your professed intention, to have confined yourself to the last. But anger has some claim to indulgence, and railing is usually a relief to the mind. I hope you have found benefit from the experiment. It is not my design to enter into a formal vindication of Mr. Grenville, upon his own principles. I have neither the honour of being personally known to him, nor do I pretend to be completely master of all the facts. I need not run the risque of doing an injustice to his opinions, or to his conduct, when your pamphlet alone carries, upon the face of it, a full vindication of both.

Your

Your first reflection is, that Mr. Grenville * was, of all men, the person, who should not have complained of inconsistence with regard to Mr. Wilkes. This, Sir, is either an unmeaning sneer, a peevish expression of resentment, or, if it means any thing, you plainly beg the question; for whether his parliamentary conduct with regard to Mr. Wilkes has or has not been inconsistent, remains yet to be proved. But it seems he received upon the spot a sufficient chastisement for exercising *so unfairly* his talents of misrepresentation. You are a lawyer, Sir, and know better than I do, upon what particular occasions a talent for misrepresentation may be *fairly* exerted; but to punish a man a second time, when he has been once sufficiently chastised, is rather too severe. It is not in the laws of England; it is not in your own commentaries, nor is it yet, I believe, in the new law you have revealed to the house of commons. I hope this doctrine has no existence but in your own heart. After all, Sir, if you had consulted that sober discretion, which you seem to oppose with triumph to the honest jollity of a

---

* Dr. Blackstone while speaking in the house had not his own excellent Commentaries in view; and Mr. Grenville, who replied to him, quoted a passage from them, which directly contradicted the doctrine maintained by the Doctor in his speech.

tavern

tavern, it might have occurred to you that, although you could have succeeded in fixing a charge of inconsistence upon Mr. Grenville, it would not have tended in any shape to exculpate yourself.

Your next insinuation, that Sir William Meredith had hastily adopted the false glosses of his new ally, is of the same sort with the first. It conveys a sneer as little worthy of the gravity of your character, as it is useless to your defence. It is of little moment to the public to enquire, by whom the charge was conceived, or by whom it was adopted. The only question we ask is, whether or no it be true. The remainder of your reflections upon Mr. Grenville's conduct destroy themselves. He could not possibly come prepared to traduce your integrity to the house. He could not foresee that you would even speak upon the question, much less could he foresee that you would maintain a direct contradiction of that doctrine, which you had solemnly, disinterestedly, and upon soberest reflection delivered to the public. He came armed indeed with what he thought a respectable authority, to support what he was convinced was the cause of truth, and I doubt not, he intended to give you, in the course of the debate, an honourable and public testimony of his esteem. Thinking highly

ly of his abilities, I cannot however allow him the gift of divination. As to what you are pleased to call a plan coolly formed to impose upon the house of commons, and his producing it without provocation at midnight, I consider it as the language of pique and invective, therefore unworthy of regard. But, Sir, I am sensible I have followed your example too long, and wandered from the point.

The quotation from your commentaries is matter of record. It can neither be *altered* by your friends, nor misrepresented by your enemies; and I am willing to take your own word for what you have said in the house of commons. If there be a real difference between what you have written and what you have spoken, you confess that your book ought to be the standard. Now, Sir, if words mean any thing, I apprehend that, when a long enumeration of disqualifications (whether by statute or the custom of parliament) concludes with these general comprehensive words, " but subject to these restric-
" tions and disqualifications, *every* subject of
" the realm is eligible of common right," a reader of plain understanding must of course rest satisfied, that no species of disqualification whatsoever had been omitted. The known character of the author, and the apparent

parent accuracy with which the whole work is compiled, would confirm him in his opinion; nor could he possibly form any other judgment, without looking upon your commentaries in the same light in which you consider those penal laws, which though not repealed, are fallen into disuse, and are now in effect A SNARE TO THE UNWARY*.

You tell us indeed that it was not part of your plan to specify any temporary incapacity, and that you could not, without a spirit of prophecy, have specified the disability of a private individual, subsequent to the period at which you wrote. What your plan was I know not; but what it should have been, in order to complete the work you have given us, is by no means difficult to determine. The incapacity, which you call temporary, may continue seven years; and though you might not have foreseen the particular case of Mr. Wilkes, you might and should have foreseen the possibility of *such* a case, and told us how far the house of commons were authorised to proceed in it by the law and custom of parliament. The freeholders of Mid-

---

* IF a Judge in stating the law upon any point, affirms that he has included every case, and it appears afterwards that he had purposely omitted a material case, he, in effect, lays *a snare for the unwary.*

dlesex

dlefex would then have known what they had to truft to, and would never have returned Mr. Wilkes, when Colonel Luttrell was a candidate againft him. They would have chofen fome indifferent perfon, rather than fubmit to be reprefented by the object of their contempt and deteftation.

Your attempt to diftinguifh between difabilities, which affect whofe claffes of men, and thofe which affect individuals only, is really unworthy of your underftanding. Your commentaries had taught me that, although the inftance, in which a penal law is exerted, be particular, the laws themfelves are general. They are made for the benefit and inftruction of the public, though the penalty falls only upon an individual. You cannot but know, Sir, that what was Mr. Wilkes's cafe yefterday may be your's or mine tomorrow, and that confequently, the common right of every fubject of the realm is invaded by it. Profeffing therefore to treat of the conftitution of the houfe of commons, and of the laws and cuftoms relative to that conftitution, you certainly were guilty of a moft unpardonable omiffion in taking no notice of a right and privilege of the houfe, more extraordinary and more arbitrary than all the others they poffefs put together. If the expulfion of a member, not under any
legal

legal difability, of itfelf creates in him an incapacity to be elected, I fee a ready way marked out, by which the majority may at any time remove the honefteft and ableft men who happen to be in oppofition to them. To fay that they *will not* make this extravagant ufe of their power, would be a language unfit for a man fo learned in the laws as you are. By your doctrine, Sir, they *have* the power, and laws you know are intended to guard againft what men *may* do, not to truft to what they *will* do.

Upon the whole, Sir, the charge againft you is of a plain, fimple nature: It appears even upon the face of your own pamphlet. On the contrary, your juftification of yourfelf is full of fubtlety and refinement, and in fome places not very intelligible. If I were perfonally your enemy, I fhould dwell, with a malignant pleafure, upon thofe great and ufeful qualifications, which you certainly poffefs, and by which you once acquired though they could not preferve to you the refpect and efteem of your country. I fhould enumerate the honours you have loft, and the virtues you have difgraced: but having no private refentments to gratify, I think it fufficient to have given my opinion of your public conduct, leaving the punifhment nishment it deserves to your closet and to yourself.

JUNIUS.

LETTER XXVIII.

TO THE PRINTER OF THE PUBLIC ADVERTISER.

SIR, 14 *August*, 1769.

A CORRESPONDENT of the St. James's Evening Post first wilfully misunderstands Junius, then censures him for a bad reasoner. Junius does not say that it was incumbent upon Doctor Blackstone to foresee and state the crimes, for which Mr. Wilkes was expelled. If, by a spirit of prophecy, he had even done so, it would have been nothing to the purpose. The question is, not for what particular offences a person may be expelled, but generally whether by the law of parliament expulsion alone creates a disqualification. If the affirmative be the law of parliament, Doctor Blackstone might and should have told us so. The question is not confined to this or that particular person, but forms one great general branch of disqualification, too important in itself, and too extensive in its consequences, to be omitted in an accurate work expressly treating of the law of parliament.

THE

The truth of the matter is evidently this, Doctor Blackstone, while he was speaking in the house of commons, never once thought of his Commentaries, until the contradiction was unexpectedly urged, and stared him in the face. Instead of defending himself upon the spot, he funk under the charge, in an agony of confusion and despair. It is well known that there was a pause of some minutes in the house, from a general expectation that the Doctor would say something in his own defence; but it seems, his faculties were too much overpowered to think of those subtleties and refinements, which have since occurred to him. It was then Mr. Grenville received that severe chastisement, which the Doctor mentions with so much triumph. *I wish the honourable gentleman, instead of shaking his head, would shake a good argument out of it.* If to the elegance, novelty, and bitterness of this ingenious sarcasm, we add the natural melody of the amiable Sir Fletcher Norton's pipe, we shall not be surprised that Mr. Grenville was unable to make him any reply.

As to the Doctor, I would recommend it to him to be quiet. If not, he may perhaps hear again from Junius himself.

PHILO JUNIUS.

POSTSCRIPT XXIX.

TO A PAMPHLET INTITLED, 'AN AN-
'SWER TO THE QUESTION STATED.'
SUPPOSED TO BE WRITTEN BY DR.
BLACKSTONE, SOLICITOR TO THE
QUEEN, IN ANSWER TO JUNIUS'S
LETTER. NO. XXV.

SINCE these papers were sent to the press, a writer in the public papers, who subscribes himself Junius, has made a feint of bringing this question to a short issue. Though the foregoing observations contain in my opinion, at least, a full refutation of all that this writer has offered, I shall, however, bestow a very few words upon him. It will cost me very little trouble to unravel and expose the sophistry of his argument.

' I TAKE the question, says he, to be strictly
' this : Whether or no it be the known esta-
' blished law of parliament, that the expulsion
' of a member of the house of commons of
' itself creates in him such an incapacity to be
' re-elected, that, at a subsequent election,
' any votes given to him are null and void;
' and that any other candidate, who, except
the

' the perfon expelled, has the greateft number
' of votes, ought to be the fitting member.'

Waving for the prefent any objection I may have to this ftate of the queftion, I fhall venture to meet our champion upon his own ground; and attempt to fupport the affirmative of it, in one of the two ways, by which he fays it can be alone fairly fupported. ' If
' there be no ftatute, fays he, in which the
' fpecific difability is clearly created, &c. (and
' we acknowledge there is none) the cuftom
' of parliament muft then be referred to, and
' fome cafe or cafes, ftrictly in point, muft
' be produced, with the decifion of the court
' upon them.' Now I affert, that this has been done. Mr. Walpole's cafe is ftrictly in point, to prove that expulfion creates abfolute incapacity of being re-elected. This was the clear decifion of the houfe upon it; and was a full declaration, that incapacity was the neceffary confequence of expulfion. The law was as clearly and firmly fixed by this refolution, and is as binding in every fubfequent cafe of expulfion, as if it had been declared by an exprefs ftatute, " That a mem-
" ber expelled by a refolution of the houfe
" of commons fhall be deemed incapable of
" being re-elected." Whatever doubt then there might have been of the law before Mr. Walpole's cafe, with refpect to the full ope-

ration of a vote of expulsion, there can be none now. The decision of the house upon this case is strictly in point to prove, that expulsion creates absolute incapacity in law of being re-elected.

But incapacity in law in this instance must have the same operation and effect with incapacity in law in every other instance. Now, incapacity of being re-elected implies in its very terms, that any votes given to the incapable person at a subsequent election are null and void. This is its necessary operation, or it has no operation at all. It is *vox et præterea nihil*. We can no more be called upon to prove this proposition, than we can to prove that a dead man is not alive, or that twice two are four. When the terms are understood, the proposition is self-evident.

Lastly, It is in all cases of election the known and established law of the land, grounded upon the clearest principles of reason and common sense, that if the votes given to one candidate are null and void, they cannot be opposed to the votes given to another candidate. They cannot affect the votes of such candidate at all. As they have, on the one hand, no positive quality to add or establish, so have they, on the other hand, no negative

gative one to fubftract or deftroy. They are, in a word, a mere non-entity. Such was the determination of the houfe of commons in the Malden and Bedford elections; cafes ftrictly in point to the prefent queftion, as far as they are meant to be in point. And to fay, that they are not in point, in all circumftances, in thofe particularly which are independent of the propofition which they are quoted to prove, is to fay no more than that Malden is not Middlefex, nor Serjeant Comyns Mr. Wilkes.

Let us fee then how our proof ftands. Expulfion creates incapacity; incapacity annihilates any votes given to the incapable perfon. The votes given to the qualified candidate ftand upon their own bottom, firm, and untouched, and can alone have effect. This, one would think, would be fufficient. But we are ftopped fhort, and told, that none of our precedents come home to the prefent cafe; and are challenged to produce " a pre-
" cedent in all the proceedings of the houfe
" of commons that does come home to it,
" viz. *where an expelled member has been re-*
" *turned again, and another candidate, with an*
" *inferior number of votes, has been declared*
" *the fitting member.*"

INSTEAD of a precedent, I will beg leave to put a cafe; which, I fancy, will be quite as decifive to the prefent point. Suppofe another Sacheverel, (and every party muft have its Sacheverel) fhould, at fome future election, take it in his head to offer himfelf a candidate for the county of Middlefex. He is oppofed by a candidate, whofe coat is of a different colour; but however of a very good colour. The divine has an indifputable majority: nay, the poor layman is abfolutely diftanced. The fheriff, after having had his confcience well informed by the reverend cafuift, returns him, as he fuppofes, duly elected. The whole houfe is in an uproar, at the apprehenfion of fo ftrange an appearance amongft them. A motion however is at length made, that the perfon was incapable of being elected, that his election therefore is null and void, and that his competitor ought to have been returned. No, fays a great orator, firft, fhew me your law for this proceeding. " Either produce me a fta-
" tute, in which the fpecific difability of a
" clergyman is created; or, produce me a
" precedent *where a clergyman has been re-*
" *turned, and another candidate, with an inferior*
" *number of votes, has been declared the fitting*
" *member.*" No fuch ftatute, no fuch precedent to be found. What anfwer then is to be given to this demand? The very fame
anfwer

answer which I will give to that of Junius: That there is more than one precedent in the proceedings of the house——" where an in- " capable person has been returned, and an- " other candidate, with an inferior number of " votes, has been declared the sitting mem- " ber; and that this is the known and esta- " blished law, in all cases of incapacity, from " whatever cause it may arise."

I SHALL now therefore beg leave to make a slight amendment to Junius's state of the question, the affirmative of which will then stand thus:

" IT is the known and established law of " parliament, that the expulsion of any mem- " ber of the house of commons creates in " him an incapacity of being re-elected; " that any votes given to him at a subse- " quent election are, in consequence of such " incapacity, null and void; and that any " other candidate, who, except the person " rendered incapable, has the greatest number " of votes, ought to be the sitting member."

BUT our business is not yet quite finished. Mr. Walpole's case must have a re-hearing. " It is not possible, says this writer, to con- " ceive a case more exactly in point. Mr. " Walpole was expelled, and having a majo- " rity

" rity of votes at the next election, was re-
" turned again. The friends of Mr. Taylor,
" a candidate set up by the ministry, peti-
" tioned the house that he might be the sitting
" member. Thus far the circumstances
" tally exactly, except that our house of
" commons saved Mr. Luttrell the trouble
" of petitioning. The point of law, how-
" ever, was the same. It came regularly be-
" fore the house, and it was their business to
" determine upon it. They did determine
" it; for they declared Mr. Taylor *not duly*
" *elected.*"

Instead of examining the justness of this representation, I shall beg leave to oppose against it my own view of this case, in as plain a manner and as few words as I am able.

It was the known and established law of parliament, when the charge against Mr. Walpole came before the house of commons, that they had power to expel, to disable, and to render incapable for offences. In virtue of this power they expelled him.

Had they, in the very vote of expulsion, adjudged him, in terms, to be incapable of being re-elected, there must have been at once an end with him. But though the right of

of the house, both to expel, and adjudge incapable, was clear and indubitable, it does not appear to me, that the full operation and effect of a vote of expulsion singly was so. The law in this case had never been expressly declared. There had been no event to call up such a declaration. I trouble not myself with the grammatical meaning of the word expulsion. I regard only its legal meaning. This was not, as I think, precisely fixed. The house thought proper to fix it, and explicitly to declare the full consequences of their former vote, before they suffered these consequences to take effect. And in this proceeding they acted upon the most liberal and solid principles of equity, justice and law. What then did the burgesses of Lynn collect from this second vote? Their subsequent conduct will tell us: it will with certainty tell us, that they considered it as decisive against Mr. Walpole; it will also, with equal certainty, tell us, that, upon supposition that the law of election stood then, as it does now, and that they knew it to stand thus, they inferred, " that at a future elec-
" tion, and in case of a similar return, the
" house would receive the same candidate, as
" duly elected, whom they had before reject-
" ed." They could infer nothing but this.

It is needless to repeat the circumstance of dissimilarity in the present case. It will be sufficient to observe, that as the law of parliament, upon which the house of commons grounded every step of their proceedings, was clear beyond the reach of doubt, so neither could the freeholders of Middlesex be at a loss to foresee what must be the Inevitable consequence of their proceedings 'in opposition to it. For upon every return of Mr. Wilkes, the house made enquiry, whether any votes were given to any other candidate?

But I could venture, for the experiment's sake, even to give this writer the utmost he asks; to allow the most perfect similarity throughout in these two cases; to allow, that the law of expulsion was quite as clear to the burgesses of Lynn, as to the freeholders of Middlesex. It will, I am confident, avail his cause but little. It will only prove, that, the law of election at that time was different from the present law. It will prove, that, in all cases of an incapable candidate returned, the law then was, that the whole election should be void. But now we know that this is not law. The cases of Malden and Bedford were, as has been seen, determined upon other and more just principles,

ples. And these determinations are, I imagine, admitted on all sides, to be law.

I WOULD willingly draw a veil over the remaining part of this paper. It is astonishing, it is painful, to see men of parts and ability, giving into the most unworthy artifices, and descending so much below their true line of character. But if they are not the dupes of their sophistry, (which is hardly to be conceived) let them consider that they are something much worse.

THE dearest interests of this country are its laws and its constitution. Against every attack upon these, there will, I hope, be always found amongst us the firmest *spirit of resistance*; superior to the united efforts of faction and ambition. For ambition, though it does not always take the lead of faction, will be sure in the end to make the most fatal advantage of it, and draw it to its own purposes. But, I trust, our day of trial is yet far off; and there is *a fund of good sense in this country, which cannot long be deceived*, by the arts either of false reasoning or false patriotism.

LETTER XXX.

TO THE PRINTER OF THE PUBLIC AD-
VERTISER.

SIR, 8 *August*, 1769.

THE gentleman, who has published an answer * to Sir William Meredith's pamphlet, having honoured me with a post-script of six quarto pages, which he moderately calls, bestowing a *very* few words upon me, I cannot, in common politeness, refuse him a reply. The form and magnitude of a quarto imposes upon the mind; and men, who are unequal to the labour of discussing an intricate argument, or wish to avoid it, are willing enough to suppose, that much has been proved, because much has been said. Mine, I confess, are humble labours. I do not presume to instruct the learned, but simply to inform the body of the people; and I prefer that channel of conveyance, which is likely to spread farthest among them. The advocates of the ministry seem to me to write for fame, and to flatter themselves, that the

* This pamphlet is entitled, " An Answer to the Question Stated."

size

size of their works will make them immortal. They pile up reluctant quarto upon solid folio, as if their labours, because they are gigantic, could contend with truth and heaven.

THE writer of the volume in question meets me upon my own ground. He acknowledges there is no statute, by which the specific disability we speak of is created, but he affirms, that the custom of parliament has been referred to, and that a case strictly in point has been produced, with the decision of the court upon it.—I thank him for coming so fairly to the point. He asserts, that the case of Mr. Walpole is strictly in point to prove that expulsion creates an absolute incapacity of being re-elected; and for this purpose he refers generally to the first vote of the house upon that occasion, without venturing to recite the vote itself. The unfair, disingenuous artifice of adopting that part of a precedent, which seems to suit his purpose, and omitting the remainder, deserves some pity, but cannot excite my resentment. He takes advantage eagerly of the first resolution, by which Mr. Walpole's incapacity is declared; but as to the two following, by which the candidate with the fewest votes was declared " not " duly elected," and the election itself vacated, I dare say he would be well satisfied,

if

if they were for ever blotted out of the journals of the house of commons. In fair argument, no part of a precedent should be admitted, unless the whole of it be given to us together. The author has divided his precedent, for he knew, that, taken together, it produced a consequence directly the reverse of that, which he endeavours to draw from a vote of expulsion. But what will this honest person say, if I take him at his word, and demonstrate to him, that the house of commons never meant to found Mr. Walpole's incapacity upon his expulsion only? What subterfuge will then remain?

Let it be remembered that we are speaking of the intention of men, who lived more than half a century ago, and that such intention can only be collected from their words and actions, as they are delivered to us upon record. To prove their designs by a supposition of what they would have done, opposed to what they actually did, is mere trifling and impertinence. The vote, by which Mr. Walpole's incapacity was declared, is thus expressed, " That Robert Walpole, Esq; hav-
" ing been this session of parliament com-
" mitted a prisoner to the Tower, and ex-
" pelled this house for a breach of trust in the
" execution of his office, and notorious cor-
" ruption when secretary at war, was and is
" in-

"incapable of being elected a member to serve in this present parliament *." Now, Sir, to my understanding, no proposition of this kind can be more evident, than that the house of commons, by this very vote, themselves understood, and meant to declare, that Mr. Walpole's incapacity arose from the crimes he had committed, not from the punishment the house annexed to them. The high breach of trust, the notorious corruption are stated in the strongest terms. They do not tell us that he was incapable because he was expelled, but because he had been guilty of such offences as justly rendered him unworthy of a seat in parliament. If they had intended to fix the disability upon his expulsion alone, the mention of his crimes in the same vote would have been highly improper. It could only perplex the minds of the electors, who, if they collected any thing from so confused a

---

* A ministerial advocate has quoted this resolution unfairly, and altered it to serve his purpose. Mr. Dyson, the compiler of that tedious quarto, entitled, *The case of the last election for the county of Middlesex considered*, has the assurance to recite this very vote, in the following terms, " *Resolved, that Robert Walpole, Esq; having been that session of parliament expelled the house, was and is incapable of being elected a member to serve in the present parliament.*" There cannot be a stronger positive proof of the treachery of the compiler, nor a stronger presumptive proof that he was convinced that the vote, if truly recited, would overturn his whole argument.

declaration of the law of parliament, must have concluded that their representative had been declared incapable because he was highly guilty, not because he had been punished. But even admitting them to have understood it in the other sense, they must then, from the very terms of the vote, have united the idea of his being sent to the Tower with that of his expulsion, and considered his incapacity as the joint effect of both *.

I do not mean to give an opinion upon the justice of the proceedings of the house of commons with regard to Mr. Walpole; but certainly, if I admitted their censure to be well founded, I could no way avoid agreeing with them in the consequence they drew from it. I could never have a doubt, in law or reason, that a man, convicted of a high breach of trust, and of a notorious corruption, in the execution of a public office, was and ought to be incapable of sitting in the same parliament. Far from attempting to invalidate that vote, I should have wished that the incapacity declared by it could legally have been continued for ever.

Now Sir, observe how forcibly the argument returns. The house of commons, upon

* See this matter farther elucidated in the letter signed Philo Junius, which immediately follows this.

the

the face of their proceedings, had the strongest motives to declare Mr. Walpole incapable of being re-elected. They thought such a man unworthy to sit among them:—To that point they proceeded no farther; for they respected the rights of the people, while they asserted their own. They did not infer, from Mr. Walpole's incapacity, that his opponent was duly elected; on the contrary they declared Mr. Taylor " Not duly elected," and the election itself void.

Such, however, is the precedent, which my honest friend assures us is strictly in point to prove, that expulsion of itself creates an incapacity of being elected. If it had been so, the present house of commons should at least have followed strictly the example before them, and should have stated to us, in the same vote, the crimes for which they expelled Mr. Wilkes; whereas they resolve simply, that, " having been expelled, he " was and is incapable." In this proceeding I am authorised to affirm, they have neither statute, nor custom, nor reason, nor one single precedent to support them. On the other side, there is indeed a precedent so strongly in point, that all the inchanted castles of ministerial magic fall before it. In the year 1698, (a period which the rankest Tory dare not except against) Mr. Wollaston

ton was expelled, re-elected, and admitted to take his feat in the same parliament. The ministry have precluded themselves from all objections drawn from the cause of his expulsion, for they affirm absolutely, that expulsion of itself creates the disability. Now, Sir, let sophistry evade, let falsehood assert, and impudence deny—here stands the precedent, a land-mark to direct us through a troubled sea of controversy, conspicuous and unremoved.

I HAVE dwelt the longer upon the discussion of this point, because, in my opinion, it comprehends the whole question. The rest is unworthy of notice. We are enquiring whether incapacity be or not be created by expulsion. In the cases of Bedford and Malden, the incapacity of the persons returned was matter of public notoriety, for it was created by act of parliament. But, really, Sir, my honest friend's suppositions are as unfavourable to him as his facts. He well knows that the clergy, besides that they are represented in common with their fellow-subjects, have also a separate parliament of their own :———that their incapacity to sit in the house of commons has been confirmed by repeated decisions of the house, and that the law of parliament, declared by those decisions, has been for above two centuries notorious

rious and undisputed. The author is certainly at liberty to fancy cases, and make whatever comparisons he thinks proper; his suppositions still continue as distant from fact, as his wild discourses are from solid argument.

The conclusion of his book is candid to extreme. He offers to grant me all I desire. He thinks he may safely admit that the case of Mr. Walpole makes directly against him, for it seems he has one grand solution *in petto* for all difficulties. *If*, says he, *I were to allow all this, it will only prove, that the law of election was different in Queen Anne's time, from what it is at present.*

This indeed is more than I expected. The principle, I know, has been maintained in fact, but I never expected to see it so formally declared. What can he mean? Does he assume this language to satisfy the doubts of the people, or does he mean to rouse their indignation; are the ministry daring enough to affirm, that the house of commons have a right to make and unmake the law of parliament at their pleasure?—Does the law of parliament, which we are so often told is the law of the land;—does the common right of every subject of the realm depend upon an arbitrary capricious vote of one
branch

branch of the legiflature?—The voice of truth and reafon muft be filent.

THE miniftry tell us plainly that this is no longer a queftion of right, but of power and force alone. What was law yefterday is not law to-day: and now it feems we have no better rule to live by than the temporary difcretion and fluctuating integrity of the houfe of commons.

PROFESSIONS of patriotifm are become ftale and ridiculous. For my own part, I claim no merit from endeavouring to do a fervice to my fellow-fubjects. I have done it to the beft of my underftanding; and, without looking for the approbation of other men, my confcience is fatisfied. What remains to be done concerns the collective body of the people. They are now to determine for themfelves, whether they will firmly and conftitutionally affert their rights; or make an humble, flavifh, furrender of them at the feet of the miniftry. To a generous mind there cannot be a doubt. We owe it to our anceftors to preferve entire thefe rights, which they have delivered to our care: we owe it to our pofterity, not to fuffer their deareft inheritance to be deftroyed. But if it were poffible for us to be infenfible of thefe facred claims, there is yet an obligation binding

ing upon ourselves, from which nothing can acquit us,—a personal interest, which we cannot surrender. To alienate even our own rights, would be a crime as much more enormous than suicide, as a life of civil security and freedom is superior to a bare existence; and if life be the bounty of heaven, we scornfully reject the noblest part of the gift, if we consent to surrender that certain rule of living, without which the condition of human nature is not only miserable, but contemptible.

JUNIUS.

LETTER XXXI.

TO THE PRINTER OF THE PUBLIC ADVERTISER.

SIR,   22 *May*, 1771.

VERY early in the debate upon the decision of the Middlesex election, it was observed by Junius, that the house of commons had not only exceeded their boasted precedent of the expulsion and subsequent incapacitation of Mr. Walpole, but that they had not even adhered to it strictly as far as it went. After convicting Mr. Dyson of giving a false quotation from the Journals, and having

having explained the purpose, which that contemptible fraud was intended to answer, he proceeds to state the vote itself, by which Mr. Walpole's supposed incapacity was declared, viz.—" Resolved, That Robert Walpole, Esq; having been this session of parliament committed a prisoner to the Tower, and expelled this house for a high breach of trust in the execution of his office, and notorious corruption when secretary at war, was and is incapable of being elected a member to serve in this present parliament:"——and then observes that, from the terms of the vote, we have no right to annex the incapacitation to the expulsion only, for that, as the proposition stands, it must arise equally from the expulsion and the commitment to the Tower. I believe, Sir, no man, who knows any thing of dialectics, or who understands English, will dispute the truth and fairness of this construction. But Junius has a great authority to support him, which, to speak with the Duke of Grafton, I accidentally met with this morning in the course of my reading. It contains an admonition, which cannot be repeated too often. Lord Sommers, in his excellent tract upon the rights of the people, after reciting the votes of the convention of the 28th of January 1689, viz.—" that King James the second, having endeavoured to
" sub-

" subvert the constitution of this kingdom
" by breaking the original contract between
" King and people, and by the advice of
" jesuits and other wicked persons having
" violated the fundamental laws, and having
" withdrawn himself out of this kingdom,
" hath abdicated the government, &c."——
makes this observation upon it. " The
" word abdicated relates to all the clauses
" aforegoing, as well as to his deserting the
" kingdom, or else they would have been
" wholly in vain." And that there might
be no pretence for confining the abdication
merely to the withdrawing, Lord Sommers
farther observes, *that King James, by refusing
to govern us according to that law, by which he
held the crown, implicitly renounced his title to
it.*

IF Junius's construction of the vote against
Mr. Walpole be now admitted, (and indeed
I cannot comprehend how it can honestly be
disputed) the advocates of the house of commons must either give up their precedent entirely, or be reduced to the necessity of maintaining one of the grossest absurdities ima-
ginable, viz. " That a commitment to the
" Tower is a constituent part of, and contri-
" butes half at least to the incapacitation of
" the person who suffers it."

Vol. I.   I   I NEED

I NEED not make you any excuse for endeavouring to keep alive the attention of the public to the decision of the Middlesex election. The more I consider it, the more I am convinced that, as a fact, it is indeed highly injurious to the rights of the people; but that, as a precedent, it is one of the most dangerous that ever was established against those who are to come after us. Yet I am so far a moderate man, that I verily believe the majority of the house of commons, when they passed this dangerous vote, neither understood the question, nor knew the consequence of what they were doing. Their motives were rather despicable, than criminal, in the extreme. One effect they certainly did not foresee. They are now reduced to such a situation, that if a member of the present house of commons were to conduct himself ever so improperly, and in reality deserve to be sent back to his constituents with a mark of disgrace, they would not dare to expel him; because they know that the people, in order to try again the great question of right, or to thwart an odious house of commons, would probably overlook his immediate unworthiness, and return the same person to parliament,—But, in time, the precedent will gain strength. A future house of commons will have no such apprehensions, consequently will not scruple to follow a precedent,

cedent, which they did not establish. The Miser himself seldom lives to enjoy the fruit of his extortion; but his heir succeeds him of course, and takes possession without censure. No man expects him to make restitution, and, no matter for his title, he lives quietly upon the estate.

PHILO JUNIUS.

LETTER XXXIII.

TO THE PRINTER OF THE PUBLIC ADVERTISER.

SIR,   22 *August*, 1769.

I MUST beg of you to print a few lines, in explanation of some passages in my last letter, which I see have been misunderstood.

1. WHEN I said, that the house of commons never meant to found Mr. Walpole's incapacity on this expulsion only, I meant no more than to deny the general proposition, that expulsion alone creates the incapacity. If there be any thing ambiguous in the expression, I beg leave to explain it by saying, that, in my opinion, expulsion neither creates,

ates, nor in any part contributes to create the incapacity in question.

2. I CAREFULLY avoided entering into the merits of Mr. Walpole's case. I did not enquire, whether the house of commons acted justly, or whether they truly declared the law of parliament. My remarks went only to their apparent meaning and intention, as it stands declared in their own resolution.

3. I NEVER meant to affirm, that a commitment to the Tower created a disqualification. On the contrary, I considered that idea as an absurdity, into which the ministry must inevitably fall, if they reasoned right upon their own principles.

THE case of Mr. Wollaston speaks for itself. The ministry assert that *expulsion alone* creates an absolute, complete incapacity to be re-elected to sit in the same parliament. This proposition they have uniformly maintained, without any condition or modification whatsoever. Mr. Wollaston was expelled, re-elected, and admitted to take his seat in the same parliament.—I leave it to the public to determine, whether this be a plain matter of fact, or mere nonsense or declamation.

JUNIUS.

LETTER

LETTER XXXIV.

TO THE PRINTER OF THE PUBLIC ADVERTISER.

4 Sept, 1769.

ARGUMENT against FACT; or, A new system of political Logic, by which the ministry have demonstrated, to the satisfaction of their friends, that expulsion alone creates a complete incapacity to be re-elected: *alias,* that a subject of this realm may be robbed of his common right, by a vote of the house of commons.

FIRST FACT.

MR. *Wollaston,* in 1698, *was expelled, re-elected, and admitted to take his seat.*

ARGUMENT.

As this cannot conveniently be reconciled with our general proposition, it may be necessary to shift our ground, and look back to the *cause* of Mr. Wollaston's expulsion. From thence it will appear clearly that, " al-
" though he was expelled, he had not ren-
" dered himself a culprit too ignominious to
" sit in parliament, and that having resigned
" his

" his employment, he was no longer inca-
" pacitated by law." *Vide Serious Considerations, page 23.* Or thus, " The house,
" somewhat *inaccurately*, used the word EX-
" PELLED; they should have called it A MO-
" TION." *Vide Mungo's case considered, page
11.* Or in short, if these arguments should
be thought insufficient, we may fairly deny
the fact. For example; " I affirm that he
" was not re-elected. The same Mr. Wol-
" laston, who was expelled, was not again
" elected. The same individual, if you
" please, walked into the house, and took his
" seat there, but the same person in law was
" not admitted a member of that parliament,
" from which he had been discarded." *Vide
Letter to Junius, page 12.*

Second Fact.

*Mr. Walpole having been committed to the
Tower, and expelled for a high breach of trust
and notorious corruption in a public office, was
declared incapable, &c.*

Argument.

From the terms of this vote, nothing can
be more evident than that the house of commons meant to fix the incapacity upon the
punishment, and not upon the crime; but
lest it should appear in a different light to
weak, uninformed persons, it may be advise-
able

able to gut the resolution, and give it to the public, with all possible solemnity, in the following terms, viz. " Resolved, that Ro-
" bert Walpole, Esq; having been that ses-
" sion of parliament expelled the house, was
" and is incapable of being elected member
" to serve in that present parliament." *Vide Mungo on the use of quotations, page* 11.

N. B. The author of the answer to Sir William Meredith seems to have made use of Mungo's quotation, for in page 18, he assures us, " That the declaratory vote of the 17th
" of February, 1769, was indeed a literal
" copy of the resolution of the house in Mr.
" Walpole's case."

Third Fact.

*His opponent, Mr. Taylor, having the small-
est number of votes at the next election, was declared* NOT DULY ELECTED.

Argument.

This fact we consider as directly in point to prove that Mr. Luttrell ought to be the sitting member, for the following reasons. " The burgesses of Lynn could draw no
" other inference from this resolution, but
" this, that at a future election, and in case
" of a similar return, the house would re-
" ceive the same candidate as duly elected,
" whom

" whom they had before rejected." *Vide Post-script to Junius*, p. 37. Or thus: " This
" their resolution leaves no room to doubt
" what part they *would* have taken, if, upon
" a subsequent re-election of Mr. Walpole,
" there had been any other candidate in com-
" petition with him. For, by their vote,
" they could have no other intention than to
" admit such other candidate." *Vide Mungo's case considered*, p. 39. Or take it in this light.—The burgesses of Lynn having, in defiance of the house, retorted upon them a person, whom they had branded with the most ignominious marks of their displeasure, were thereby so well intitled to favour and indulgence, that the house could do no less than rob Mr. Taylor of a right legally vested in him, in order that the burgesses might be apprised of the law of parliament; which law, the house took a very direct way of explaining to them, by resolving that the candidate with the fewest votes was not duly elected:—" And was not this much more
" equitable, more in the spirit of that equal
" and substantial justice, which is the end of
" all law, than if they had violently adhered
" to the strict maxims of law?". *Vide Serious Considerations*, p. 33 *and* 34. " And if the
" present house of commons had chosen to
" follow the spirit of this resolution, they
" would have received and established the
" can-

" candidate with the fewest votes." *Vide Answer to Sir William Meredith, p. 18.*

PERMIT me now, Sir, to shew you that the worthy Dr. Blackstone sometimes contradicts the ministry as well as himself. The Speech without doors asserts, page 9, " that " the legal effect of an incapacity, founded " on a judicial determination of a complete " court, is precisely the same as that of an " incapacity created by act of parliament." Now for the Doctor—*The law and the opinion of the judge are not always convertible terms, or one and the same thing; since it sometimes may happen that the judge may mistake the law.* Commentaries, Vol. I. p. 71.

THE answer to Sir William Meredith asserts, page 23, " That the returning of- " ficer is not a judicial, but a purely mi- " nisterial officer. His return is no judicial " act."—At 'em again Doctor. *The Sheriff, in his judicial capacity, is to hear and determine causes of 40 shillings value and under in his county court. He has also a judicial power in divers other civil cases. He is likewise to decide the elections of knights of the shire (subject to the control of the house of commons), to judge of the qualification of voters, and to return such as he shall* DETERMINE *to be duly elected.* Vide Commentaries, page 332. Vol. I.

WHAT conclusion shall we draw from such facts, and such arguments, such contradictions? I cannot express my opinion of the present ministry more exactly than in the words of Sir Richard Steele, "*that we are governed by a set of drivellers, whose folly takes away all dignity from distress, and makes even calamity ridiculous.*"

PHILO JUNIUS.

The following curious letter is omitted in the author's own edition. The double entendre though very delicately carried forward, was perhaps thought an improper subject to be classed with grave political matter.

LETTER XXXV.

TO THE PRINTER OF THE PUBLIC ADVERTISER.

SIR,

I FIND myself unexpectedly married in the newspapers, without my knowledge or consent. Since I am fated to be a husband, I hope at least the lady will perform the principal duty of a wife. Marriages, they say,

say, are made in heaven, but they are consummated upon earth; and since Junia* has adopted my name, she cannot, in common matrimonial decency, refuse to make me a tender of her person. Politics are too barren a subject for a new-married couple. I should be glad to furnish her with one more fit for a lady to handle, and better suited to the natural dexterity of her sex. In short, if Junia be young and handsome, she will have no reason to complain of my method of conducting an argument. I abominate all tergiversation in discourse, *and she may be assured that whatever I advance, whether it be weak or forcible, shall, at any rate, be directly in point.* It is true I am a strenuous advocate for liberty and property, but when these rights are invaded by a pretty woman, I am neither able to defend my money nor my freedom. The divine right of beauty is the only one an Englishman ought to acknowledge, and a pretty woman the only tyrant he is not authorised to resist.

JUNIUS.

* THE signature of a letter in the papers.

LETTER XXXVI.

TO HIS GRACE THE DUKE OF BEDFORD.

MY LORD,   19 Sept. 1769.

YOU are so little accustomed to receive any marks of respect or esteem from the public, that, if in the following lines, a compliment or expression of applause should escape me, I fear you would consider it as a mockery of your established character, and perhaps an insult to your understanding. You have nice feelings, my Lord, if we may judge from your resentments. Cautious therefore of giving offence, where you have so little deserved it, I shall leave the illustration of your virtues to other hands. Your friends have a privilege to play upon the easiness of your temper, or possibly they are better acquainted with your good qualities than I am. You have done good by stealth. The rest is upon record. You have still left ample room for speculation, when panegyric is exhausted.

You are indeed a very considerable man. The highest rank;—a splendid fortune; and a name glorious till it was yours, were sufficient to have supported you with meaner abilities

abilities than I think you possess. From the first, you derive a constitutional claim to respect; from the second, a natural extensive authority;—the last created a partial expectation of hereditary virtues. The use you have made of these uncommon advantages might have been more honourable to yourself, but could not be more instructive to mankind. We may trace it in the veneration of your country, the choice of your friends, and in the accomplishment of every sanguine hope, which the public might have conceived from the illustrious name of Russel.

THE eminence of your station gave you a commanding prospect of your duty. The road, which led to honour, was open to your view. You could not lose it by mistake, and you had no temptation to depart from it by design. Compare the natural dignity, and importance of the richest peer of England;—the noble independence, which he might have maintained in parliament, and the real interest and respect, which he might have acquired, not only in parliament, but through the whole kingdom; compare these glorious distinctions, with the ambition of holding a share in government, the emoluments of a place, the sale of a borough, or the purchase of a corporation; and though you may not regret the virtues, which create
respect,

respect, you may see with anguish, how much real importance and authority you have lost. Consider the character of an independent, virtuous Duke of Bedford; imagine what he might be in this country, then reflect one moment upon what you are. If it be possible for me to withdraw my attention from the fact, I will tell you in theory what such a man might be.

CONSCIOUS of his own weight and importance, his conduct in parliament would be directed by nothing but the constitutional duty of a peer. He would consider himself as a guardian of the laws. Willing to support the just measures of government, but determined to observe the conduct of the minister with suspicion, he would oppose the violence of faction with as much firmness, as the encroachments of prerogative. He would be as little capable of bargaining with the minister for places for himself, or his dependants, as of descending to mix himself in the intrigues of opposition. Whenever an important question called for his opinion in parliament, he would be heard, by the most profligate minister, with deference and respect. His authority would either sanctify or disgrace the measures of government.—The people would look up to him as to their protector, and a virtuous prince would have one honest

honest man in his dominions, in whose integrity and judgment he might safely confide. If it should be the will of providence to afflict him with a domestic misfortune*, he would submit to the stroke, with feeling, but not without dignity. He would consider the people as his children, and receive a generous heart-felt consolation, in the sympathising tears, and blessings of his country.

Your Grace may probably discover something more intelligible in the negative part of this illustrious character. The man I have described would never prostitute his dignity in parliament by an indecent violence either in opposing or defending a minister. He would not at one moment rancorously perse-

---

* The Duke had lately lost his only son, Francis Marquis of Tavistock. The horse of this amiable young nobleman fell under him in leaping a low hedge as he was returning from a fox chase, and in struggling to rise trampled on the Marquis's head, and fractured his skull. The Marquis died of the wound, March 22d, 1767, universally lamented. He was in the 28th year of his age. His excellent consort, Elizabeth, the daughter of William Anne, Earl of Albemarle, and sister to the present Admiral Keppel, being inconsolable for her loss, languished about a year and an half, and died Nov. 2d, 1768. At her death, she was also in the 28th year of her age. The Marquis had two sons by this lady; the eldest, Francis, now Duke of Bedford, was born Aug. 11, 1765.

cute

cute, at another basely cringe to the favourite
of his Sovereign. After outraging the royal
dignity with, peremptory conditions, little
short of menace and hostility, he would never descend to the humility of soliciting an
interview,* with the favourite, and of offer-
ing to recover, at any price, the honour of
his friendship. Though deceived perhaps in
his youth, he would not, through the course
of a long life, have invariably chosen his
friends from among the most profligate of
mankind. His own honour would have forbidden him from mixing his private pleasures
or conversation with jockeys, gamesters,
blasphemers, gladiators, or buffoons. He
would then have never felt, much less would
he have submitted to the dishonest necessity,
of engaging in the interests and intrigues of
his dependents, of supplying their vices, or
relieving their beggary, at the expence of his
country. He would not have betrayed such
ignorance, or such contempt of the constitution, as openly to avow, in a court of justice,
the † purchase and sale of a borough. He

---

* IT is said the Duke solicited this interview. The parties met at the late Earl of Eglingtouns, but Lord Bute
declared to the Duke, that he would never have any more
connexion with a man who had already betrayed him.

† His Grace, for a certain sum, had promised to return a gentleman to parliament for one of his Boroughs. A suit was brought against him for the recovery of the money, and he was obliged to repay it.

would

would not have thought it confiftent with his rank in the ftate, or even with his perfonal importance, to be the little tyrant of a little corporation †. He would never have been infulted with virtues, which he had laboured to extinguifh, nor fuffered the difgrace of a mortifying defeat, which has made him ridiculous and contemptible, even to the few by whom he was not detefted.—I reverence the afflictions of a good man,—his forrows are facred. But how can we take part in the diftreffes of a man, whom we can neither love nor efteem; or feel for a calamity, of which he himfelf is infenfible? Where was the father's heart, when he could look for, or find an immediate confolation for the lofs of an only fon, in confultations and bargains for a place at court, and even in the mifery of balloting at the India Houfe!

Admitting then that you have miftaken or deferted thofe honourable principles, which ought to have directed your conduct; admitting that you have as little claim to private affection as to public efteem, let us fee with

† The Corporation of Bedford entertained fuch a diflike to his affumed patronage, that they admitted a number of ftrangers to the freedom of that town, and totally fhook off his Grace. The public cannot have forgot the excurfions of numbers of people from London, in order to be made free of that corporation.

what

what abilities, with what degree of judgment you have carried your own system into execution. A great man, in the success and even in the magnitude of his crimes, finds a rescue from contempt. Your Grace is every way unfortunate. Yet I will not look back to those ridiculous scenes, by which in your earlier days, you thought it an honour to be distinguished.*;—the recorded stripes, the public infamy, your own sufferings, or Mr. Rigby's fortitude. These events undoubtedly left an impression, though not upon your mind. To such a mind, it may perhaps be a pleasure to reflect, that there is hardly a corner of any of his Majesty's kingdoms, ex-

* Mr. Humphreys, an Attorney, attacked his Grace with his horsewhip at Litchfield Races with great severity. He was rescued by the vigour and intrepidity of Mr. Rigby. This was a dangerous service, for Mr. Humphreys was strongly supported. This generous interposition occasioned the after close connection between his Grace and Mr. Rigby. The following stroke of Lord Chesterfield has greatly assisted to keep alive his Grace's Litchfield adventure. Sir Edward Hawke, in his official letter, after defeating the French Fleet in 1747, said, that the French ships being large took a great deal of DRUBBING; his Majesty not understanding the word, asked Lord Chesterfield to explain it; but his Lordship seeing the Duke of Bedford, at that instant, enter the closet, referred the King to his Grace, as a nobleman much more able to do it, from having felt it experimentally.

cept France, in which, at one time or other, your valuable life has not been in danger. Amiable man! we see and acknowledge the protection of Providence, by which you have so often escaped the personal detestation of your fellow subjects, and are still reserved for the public justice of your country.

Your history begins to be important at that auspicious period, at which you were deputed to represent the Earl of Bute, at the court of Versailles. It was an honourable office, and executed with the same spirit, with which it was accepted. Your patrons wanted an ambassador, who would submit to make concessions, without daring to insist upon any honourable condition for his Sovereign. Their business required a man, who had as little feeling for his own dignity as for the welfare of his country; and they found him in the first rank of the nobility. Belleisle, Goree, Guadeloupe, St. Lucia, Martinique, the Fishery, and the Havannah, are glorious monuments of your Grace's talents for negociation. My Lord, we are too well acquainted with your pecuniary character, to think it possible that so many public sacrifices should have been made, without some private compensations. Your conduct carries with it an internal evidence, beyond all the legal proofs of a court of justice.

Even

Even the callous pride of Lord Egremont *
was alarmed. He saw and felt his own diſho-
nour in correſponding with you; and there
certainly was a moment, at which he meant
to have reſiſted, had not a fatal lethargy prevailed over his faculties, and carried all ſenſe
and memory away with it.

I will not pretend to ſpecify the ſecret
terms on which you were invited to ſupport
an adminiſtration † which Lord Bute pretended to leave in full poſſeſſion of their mi-
niſterial authority, and perfectly maſters of
themſelves. He was not of a temper to relin-
quiſh power, though he retired from employment. Stipulations were certainly made
between your Grace and him, and certainly
violated. After two years ſubmiſſion, you
thought you had collected a ſtrength ſuffi-
cient to controul his influence, and that it was
your turn to be a tyrant, becauſe you had
been a ſlave. When you found yourſelf miſ-
taken in your opinion of your gracious Maſ-
ter's firmneſs, diſappointment got the better

---

* THE Earl of Egremont, when his Grace was
negociating the Peace of Paris, wrote a letter to him,
which gave ſuch offence, that the Duke wrote to be
recalled. It has been ſaid, that it coſt Lord Bute ſome
trouble to pacify him.

† THE Grenville Adminiſtration.

of all your humble discretion, and carried you to an excess of outrage to his person ‡, as distant from true spirit, as from all decency and respect. After robbing him of the rights of a King, you would not permit him to preserve the honour of a gentleman. It was then Lord Weymouth was nominated to Ireland, and dispatched (we well remember with what indecent hurry) to plunder the treasury of the first fruits of an employment which you well knew he was never to execute ‖.

This sudden declaration of war against the favourite might have given you a momentary merit with the public, if it had either been adopted upon principle, or maintained with resolution. Without looking back to all your former servility, we need only ob-

‡ When Mr. Grenville attempted to exclude the Princess Dowager out of the Regency, his dismission was determined upon. When the Duke was informed of this, he asked an audience of a certain person, reproached him in the grossest manner, and it was declared, shocked his sensibility to such a degree, as to leave him in convulsions.

‖ Lord Weymouth did not go to Ireland, but he received three thousand pounds for plate and equipage, which are always issued as soon as the appointment is made.

serve

serve your subsequent conduct, to see upon what motives you acted. Apparently united with Mr. Grenville, you waited until Lord Rockingham's feeble administration should dissolve in its own weakness.—The moment their dismission was suspected, the moment you perceived that another system was adopted in the closet, you thought it no disgrace to return to your former dependance, and solicit once more the friendship of Lord Bute. You begged an interview, at which he had spirit enough to treat you with contempt.

It would now be of little use to point out, by what a train of weak, injudicious measures, it became necessary, or was thought so, to call you back to a share in the administration. The friends, whom you did not in the last instance desert, were not of a character to add strength or credit to government; and at that time your alliance with the Duke of Grafton was, I presume, hardly foreseen. We must look for other stipulations, to account for that sudden resolution of the closet, by which three of your dependants * (whose characters, I think, cannot be less respected than they are)

* Lord Gower, Viscount Weymouth, and Earl of Sandwich. Lord Gower is now the head of the Bedford party. Lord Sandwich set up for himself after the death of the Duke. Witness Lord Gower's support of Admiral Keppel against Lord Sandwich.

were

were advanced to offices, through which you might again controul the minister, and probably engross the whole direction of affairs.

The possession of absolute power is now once more within your reach. The measures you have taken to obtain and confirm it, are too gross to escape the eyes of a discerning judicious prince. His palace is besieged; the lines of circumvallation are drawing round him; and unless he finds a resource in his own activity, or in the attachment of the real friends of his family, the best of princes must submit to the confinement of a state prisoner, until your Grace's death, or some less fortunate event shall raise the siege. For the present, you may safely resume that stile of insult and menace, which even a private gentleman cannot submit to hear without being contemptible. Mr. Mackenzie's history is not yet forgotten, and you may find precedents enough of the mode, in which an imperious subject may signify his pleasure to his Sovereign. Where will this gracious monarch look for assistance, when the wretched Grafton could forget his obligations to his master, and desert him for a hollow alliance with *such* a man as the Duke of Bedford.

Let us consider you, then, as arrived at the summit of worldly greatness: let us suppose,

pose, that all your plans of avarice and ambition are accomplished, and your most sanguine wishes gratified in the fear, as well as the hatred of the people: Can age itself forget that you are now in the last act of life? Can grey hairs make folly venerable? and is there no period to be reserved for meditation and retirement? For shame! my Lord: let it not be recorded of you, that the latest moments of your life were dedicated to the same unworthy pursuits, the same busy agitations, in which your youth and manhood were exhausted. Consider, that, although you cannot disgrace your former life, you are violating the character of age, and exposing the impotent imbecility, after you have lost the vigour of the passions.

YOUR friends will ask, perhaps, Whither shall this unhappy old man retire? Can he remain in the metropolis, where his life has been so often threatened, and his palace so often attacked? If he returns to Wooburn*, scorn and mockery await him. He must create a solitude round his estate, if he would avoid the face of reproach and derision. At Plymouth, his destruction would be more than probable; at Exeter, inevitable. No honest Englishman will ever forget his attachment,

---

* THE Duke's seat in Bedfordshire.

nor

nor any honest Scotchman forgive his treachery to Lord Bute. At every town he enters, he must change his liveries and name. Which ever way he flies, the *Hue and Cry* of the country pursues him.

IN another kingdom indeed, the blessings of his administration have been more sensibly felt; his virtues better understood; or at worst, they will not, for him alone, forget their hospitality.—As well might VERRES have returned to Italy. You have twice escaped, my Lord: beware of a third experiment. The indignation of a whole people, plundered, insulted, and oppressed as they have been, will not be always disappointed.

IT is in vain therefore to shift the scene. You can no more fly from your enemies than from yourself. Persecuted abroad, you look into your own heart for consolation, and find nothing but reproaches and despair. But, my Lord, you may quit the field of business, though not the field of danger; and though you cannot be safe, you may cease to be ridiculous. I fear you have listened too long to the advice of those pernicious friends, with whose interests you have sordidly united your own, and for whom you have sacrificed every thing that ought to be dear to a man of honour. They are still base enough to encourage the follies of your age, as they once did the vices of your youth. As little acquainted with the rules of decorum, as with the laws of morality, they will not suffer you to profit by experience, nor even to consult the propriety of a bad character. Even now they tell you, that life is no more than a dramatic scene, in which the hero should preserve his consistency to the last, and that as you lived without virtue, you should die * without repentance.

JUNIUS.

* His Grace survived the publication of this letter about fourteen months. He died, January 15th, 1771, in the 61st year of his age, at his house in Bloomsbury Square.

LETTER XXXVII.

SIR WILLIAM DRAPER * TO JUNIUS.

SIR,   14 *September*, 1769.

HAVING accidentally feen a *republication* of your letters, wherein you have been pleafed to *affert*, that I had fold the companions of my fuccefs; I am again obliged to declare the faid affertion to be a moft *infamous* and *malicious falfehood*; and I *again* call upon you to ftand forth, avow yourfelf, and *prove* the charge. If you can make it out to the fatisfaction of any one man in the kingdom, I will be content to be thought the worft man in it; if you do not, what muft the nation think of you? *Party* has nothing to do in this affair: you have made a perfonal attack upon my honour, defamed me by a moft vile calumny, which might poffibly have funk into oblivion, had not fuch uncommon

---

* SIR WILLIAM DRAPER, having been ftopped in his career of writing in defence of the Marquis of Granby, by the Marquis himfelf, in the above letter, opens the conteft on his own account. Junius by the motto to his reply, feems to hint, and very juftly, that his former animadverfions continued to rankle in Sir William's mind.

pains been taken to renew and perpetuate this scandal, chiefly because it has been told in good language: for I give you full credit for your elegant diction, well turned periods, and attic wit; but wit is oftentimes false, though it may appear brilliant; which is exactly the case of your *whole performance*. But, Sir, I am obliged in the most *serious* manner to accuse you of being guilty of *falsities*. You have said the thing that is *not*. To support your story, you have recourse to the following *irresistible* argument: " You *sold* the companions " of your victory, because when the 16th regi- " ment was given to *you*, you was *silent*." The conclusion is inevitable. I believe that such *deep* and *acute reasoning* could only come from such an extraordinary writer as *Junius*. But unfortunately for you, the *premises* as well as the *conclusion* are absolutely *false*. Many applications have been made to the ministry on the subject of the Manilla Ransom *since* the time of my being colonel of that regiment. As I have for some years quitted London, I was obliged to have recourse to the honourable Colonel Monson and Sir Samuel Cornish to *negotiate* for me; in the last autumn, I personally delivered a memorial to the Earl of Shelburne at his seat in Wiltshire. As you have told us of your importance, that you are a person of *rank* and *fortune*, and above a *common bribe*, you may in all probability be

not

not *unknown* to his lordship, who can satisfy you of the truth of what I say. But I shall now take the liberty, Sir, to seize your battery, and turn it against yourself. If your puerile and tinsel logic could carry the least weight or conviction with it, how must you stand affected by the *inevitable conclusion*, as you are pleased to term it? According to *Junius, Silence* is *Guilt*. In many of the public papers, you have been called in the most direct and offensive terms a *liar* and a *coward*. When did you reply to these foul accusations? You have been quite *silent*; quite chop-fallen: therefore *because* you was *silent*, the nation has a right to pronounce you to be both a liar and a coward from your own argument: but, Sir, I will give you fair play; will afford you an opportunity to wipe off the first appellation; by desiring the proofs of your charge against me. Produce them! To wipe off the last, produce *yourself*. People cannot bear any longer your *Lion's skin*, and the despicable *imposture* of the *old Roman name* which you have *affected*. For the future assume the name of some *modern* * bravo and dark assassin: let your appellation have some affinity to your practice. But if I must *perish*,

---

* FROM the above expression, one would imagine that Sir William thought Brutus an *ancient* bravo and dark assassin.

Junius,

Junius, let me *perish* in the face of day; be for *once* a generous and open enemy. I allow that gothic *appeals* to cold iron are no better proofs of a man's honesty and veracity than hot iron and burning ploughshares are of *female chastity:* but a soldier's honour is as delicate as a woman's; it must not be suspected; you have dared to throw more than a suspicion upon mine: you cannot but know the consequences, which even the meekness of Christianity would pardon me for, after the injury you have done me.

WILLIAM DRAPER.

LETTER XXXVIII.

Hæret lateri lethalis arundo.

TO SIR WILLIAM DRAPER, K. B.

SIR,   25 *September*, 1769.

AFTER so long an interval, I did not expect to see the debate revived between us. My answer to your last letter shall be short; for I write to you with reluctance, and I hope we shall now conclude our correspondence for ever.

HAD

Had you been originally and without provocation attacked by an anonymous writer, you would have had some right to demand his name. But in this cause you are a volunteer. You engaged in it with the unpremeditated gallantry of a soldier. You were content to set your name in opposition to a man, who would probably continue in concealment. You understood the terms upon which we were to correspond, and gave at least a tacit assent to them. After voluntarily attacking me under the character of Junius, what possible right have you to know me under any other? Will you forgive me if I insinuate to you, that you foresaw some honour in the apparent spirit of coming forward in person, and that you were not quite indifferent to the display of your literary qualifications?

You cannot but know that the republication of my letters was no more than a catch-penny contrivance of a printer, in which it was impossible I should be concerned, and for which I am no way answerable. At the same time I wish you to understand, that if I do not take the trouble of reprinting these papers, it is not from any fear of giving offence to Sir William Draper.

Your remarks upon a signature, adopted merely for distinction, are unworthy of notice;

tice; but when you tell me I have submitted to be called a liar and a coward, I must ask you in my turn, whether you seriously think it any way incumbent upon me to take notice of the silly invectives of every simpleton, who writes in a news-paper; and what opinion you would have conceived of my discretion, if I had suffered myself to be the dupe of so shallow an artifice?

Your appeal to the sword, though consistent enough with your late profession, will neither prove your innocence nor clear you from suspicion.——Your complaints with regard to the Manilla ransom were, for a considerable time, a distress to government. You were appointed (greatly out of your turn) to the command of a regiment, and *during that administration* we heard no more of Sir William Draper. The facts, of which I speak, may indeed be variously accounted for, but they are too notorious to be denied; and I think you might have learnt at the university, that a false conclusion is an error in argument, not a breach of veracity. Your solicitations, I doubt not, were renewed under another administration. Admitting the fact, I fear an indifferent person would only infer from it, that experience had made you acquainted with the benefits of complaining. Remember, Sir, that you have yourself confessed

fessed, that, *considering the critical situation of this country, the ministry are in the right to temporise with Spain.* This confession reduces you to an unfortunate dilemma. By renewing your solicitations, you must either mean to force your country into a war at a most unseasonable juncture; or, having no view or expectation of that kind, that you look for nothing but a private compensation to yourself.

As to me, it is by no means necessary that I should be exposed to the resentment of the worst and the most powerful men in this country, though I may be indifferent about yours. Though *you* would fight, there are others who would assassinate.

But after all, Sir, where is the injury? You assure me, that my logic is puerile and tinsel, that it carries not the least weight or conviction, that my premises are false and my conclusions absurd. If this be a just description of me, how is it possible for such a writer to disturb your peace of mind, or to injure a character so well established as yours? Take care, Sir William, how you indulge this unruly temper, lest the world should suspect that conscience has some share in your resentments. You have more to fear from the treachery of your own passions, than from any malevolence of mine.

I BELIEVE, Sir, you will never know me. A confiderable time muft certainly elapfe before we are perfonally acquainted. You need not, however, regret the delay, or fuffer an apprehenfion that any length of time can reftore you to the Chriftian meeknefs of your temper, and difappoint your prefent indignation. If I underftand your character, there, is in your own breaft a repofitory, in which your refentments may be fafely laid up for future occafions, and preferved without the hazard of diminution. The *Odia in longum jaciens, quæ reconderet, auctaque promeret,* I thought had only belonged to the worft character of antiquity. The text is in Tacitus;—you know beft where to look for the commentary.

JUNIUS.

LETTER XXXIX.

FROM SIR WILLIAM DRAPER. A WORD AT PARTING TO JUNIUS*.

SIR, 7 *October*, 1769.

AS you have not favoured me with either of the *explanations* demanded of you, I can have nothing more to say to you upon my *own* account. Your mercy to me, or tenderness for yourself, has been very great. The public will judge of your *motives*. If your excess of modesty forbids you to produce either the proofs or yourself, I will excuse it. Take courage, I have not the temper of Tiberius, any more than the rank or power. You, indeed, are a tyrant of another sort, and upon your political bed of torture can excruciate any subject, from a first minister down to such a grub or butterfly as myself; like another detested tyrant of antiquity, can make the wretched sufferer fit

---

* SIR WILLIAM was on the eve of his departure to the continent of British America. Junius had the honour of sending him on his travels. Four days after the date of this letter he agreed with a Bristol Trader, for his passage to South Carolina.

the bed, if the bed will not fit the sufferer, by disjointing or tearing the trembling limbs until they are stretched to its extremity. But courage, constancy, and patience, under torments, have sometimes caused the most hardened monsters to relent, and forgive the object of their cruelty. You, Sir, are determined to try all that human nature can endure, until she expires: else, was it possible that you could be the author of that most inhuman letter to the Duke of Bedford, I have read with astonishment and horror? Where, Sir, where were the feelings of your own heart, when you could upbraid a most affectionate father with the loss of his only and most amiable son? Read over again those cruel lines of yours, and let them wring your very soul! Cannot political questions be discussed without descending to the most odious personalities?* Must you go wantonly

out

---

* MODERN degeneracy is not to be touched or reformed by meek censures. Political as well as moral offenders must smart under the lash. Mr. Pope, in his letter, dated July 26th, 1734, to Dr. Arbuthnot, says, with truth on his side, that " To reform and not to " chastise, I am afraid, is impossible; and that the " best precepts, as well as the best laws, would prove " of small use, if there were no examples to enforce " them. To attack vices in the abstract, without " touching persons, may be safe fighting indeed, but " it is fighting with shadows. My greatest comfort

" and

out of your way to torment declining age, because the Duke of Bedford may have quarrelled with those whose cause and politics you espouse? For shame! for shame! As you have *spoke daggers* to him, you may justly dread the *use* of them against your own breast, did a want of courage or of noble sentiments stimulate him to such mean revenge. He is above it; he is brave. Do you fancy that your own base arts have infected our whole island? But your own reflections, your own conscience, must and will, if you have any spark of humanity remaining, give him most ample vengeance. Not all the power of words with which you are so graced, will ever wash out, or even palliate this foul blot in your character. I have not time at present to dissect your letter so minutely as I could wish, but I will be bold enough to say, that it is (as to reason and argument) the most extraordinary piece of *florid impotence* that was ever imposed upon the eyes and ears of the too credulous and deluded mob. It accuses the Duke of Bedford of high treason. Upon what foundation? You tell us, "that "the Duke's *pecuniary character* makes it "more than *probable*, that he could not have "made such sacrifices at the peace, without

"and encouragment to proceed has been to see that "those, who have no shame, and no fear of any thing "else, have appeared touched by my satires."

" *some*

" *some private compensations* ; that his conduct
" carried with it an interior evidence, be-
" yond all the legal proofs of a court of
" justice."

My academical education, Sir, bids me tell you that it is necessary to establish the truth of your first proposition, before you presume to draw inferences from it. First prove the avarice, before you make the rash, hasty, and most wicked conclusion. This father, *Junius*, whom you call avaricious, allowed that son eight thousand pounds a year. Upon his most unfortunate death, which your usual good-nature took care to remind him of, he greatly increased the jointure of the afflicted lady, his widow. Is this avarice? Is this doing good by *stealth?* It is upon record.

If exact order, method, and true œconomy as a master of a family; if splendor and just magnificence, without wild waste and thoughtless extravagance, may constitute the character of an avaricious man, the Duke is guilty. But for a moment let us admit that an ambassador may love money too much; what proof do you give that he has taken any to betray his country? Is it hearsay; or the evidence of letters, or ocular; or the evidence of those concerned in this black affair?

Pro-

Produce your authorities to the public. It is a moſt impudent kind of ſorcery to attempt to blind us with the ſmoke, without convincing us that the fire has exiſted. You firſt brand him with a vice that he is free from, to render him odious and ſuſpected. Suſpicion is the foul weapon with which you make all your chief attacks; with that you ſtab. But ſhall one of the firſt ſubjects of the realm be ruined in his fame; ſhall even his life be in conſtant danger, from a charge built upon ſuch ſandy foundations? Muſt his houſe be beſieged by lawleſs ruffians, his journies impeded, and even the aſylum of an altar be inſecure, from aſſertions ſo baſe and falſe? Potent as he is, the Duke is amenable to juſtice; if guilty, puniſhable. The parliament is the high and ſolemn tribunal for matters of ſuch great moment. To that be they ſubmitted. But I hope alſo that ſome notice will be taken of, and ſome puniſhment inflicted upon falſe accuſers, eſpecially upon ſuch, *Junius*, who are *wilfully falſe*. In any truth I will agree even with *Junius*; will agree with him that it is highly unbecoming the dignity of Peers to tamper with boroughs. Ariſtocracy is as fatal as democracy. Our conſtitution admits of neither. It loves a King, Lords, and Commons really choſen by the unbought ſuffrages of a free people. But if corruption only ly shifts hands; if the wealthy commoner gives the bribe, instead of the potent Peer, is the state better served by this exchange? Is the real emancipation of the borough effected, because new parchment bonds may possibly supersede the old? To say the truth, wherever such practices prevail, they are equally criminal to and destructive of our freedom.

THE rest of your declamation is scarce worth considering, excepting for the elegance of the language. Like Hamlet in the play, you produce two pictures; you tell us, that one is not like the Duke of Bedford: then you bring a most hideous caricatura, and tell us of the resemblance; but *multum abludit imago.*

ALL your long tedious accounts of the ministerial quarrels, and the intrigues of the cabinet, are reducible to a few short lines; and to convince you, Sir, that I do not mean to flatter any minister, either past or present, these are my thoughts: they seem to have acted like lovers, or children; have pouted, quarrelled, cried, kissed, and been friends again, as the objects of desire, the ministerial rattles *, have been put into their hands. But such

---

* SIR WILLIAM's own account of the behaviour of the Duke and his friends, the men, according to him the best

such proceedings are very unworthy of the gravity and dignity of a great nation. We do not want men of abilities; but we have wanted steadiness; we want unanimity: your letters, *Junius*, will not contribute thereto. You may one day expire by a flame of your own kindling. But it is my humble opinion that lenity and moderation, pardon and oblivion, will disappoint the efforts of all the seditious in the land, and extinguish their wide spreading fires. I have lived with this sentiment; with this I shall die.

WILLIAM DRAPER.

LETTER XL.

TO THE PRINTER OF THE PUBLIC ADVERTISER.

SIR,   13 *October*, 1769.

IF Sir William Draper's bed be a bed of torture, he has made it for himself. I shall never interrupt his repose. Having changed the subject, there are parts of his last letter not undeserving of a reply. Leaving his private character and conduct out of the question, I shall consider him merely in

best qualified to govern the empire, shews them in a light perfectly ridiculous.

the

the capacity of an author, whose labours certainly do no discredit to a news-paper.

We say, in common discourse, that a man may be his own enemy, and the frequency of the fact makes the expression intelligible. But that a man should be the bitterest enemy of his friends, implies a contradiction of a peculiar nature. There is something in it, which cannot be conceived without a confusion of ideas, nor expressed without a solecism in language. Sir William Draper is still that fatal friend Lord Granby found him. Yet I am ready to do justice to his generosity; if indeed it be not something more than generous, to be the voluntary advocate of men, who think themselves injured by his assistance, and to consider nothing in the cause he adopts, but the difficulty of defending it. I thought however he had been better read in the history of the human heart, than to compare or confound the tortures of the body with those of the mind. He ought to have known, though perhaps it might not be his interest to confess, that no outward tyranny can reach the mind. If conscience plays the tyrant, it would be greatly for the benefit of the world that she were more arbitrary, and far less placable, than some men find her.

But

But it seems I have outraged the feelings of a father's heart.—Am I indeed so injudicious? Does Sir William Draper think I would have hazarded my credit with a generous nation, by so gross a violation of the laws of humanity? Does he think I am so little acquainted with the first and noblest characteristic of Englishmen? Or how will he reconcile such folly with an understanding so full of artifice as mine? Had he been a father, he would have been but little offended with the severity of the reproach, for his mind would have been filled with the justice of it. He would have seen that I did not insult the feelings of a father, but the father who felt nothing. He would have trusted to the evidence of his own paternal heart, and boldly denied the possibility of the fact, instead of defending it. Against whom then will his honest indignation be directed, when I assure him, that this whole town beheld the Duke of Bedford's conduct, upon the death of his son, with horror and astonishment. Sir William Draper does himself but little honour in opposing the general sense of his country. The people are seldom wrong in their opinions—in their sentiments they are never mistaken. There may be a vanity perhaps in a singular way of thinking;—but when a man professes a want of those feelings, which do honour to the multitude,

he

he hazards something infinitely more important than the character of his understanding. After all, as Sir William may possibly be in earnest in his anxiety for the Duke of Bedford, I should be glad to relieve him from it. He may rest assured this worthy nobleman laughs, with equal indifference, at my reproaches, and Sir William's distress about him. But here let it stop. Even the Duke of Bedford, insensible as he is, will consult the tranquility of his life, in not provoking the moderation of my temper. If, from the profoundest contempt, I should ever rise into anger, he should soon find, that all I have already said of him was lenity and compassion.

Out of a long catalogue, Sir William Draper has confined himself to the refutation of two charges only. The rest he had not time to discuss; and indeed it would have been a laborious undertaking. To draw up a defence of such a series of enormities, would have required a life at least as long as that, which has been uniformly employed in the practice of them. The public opinion of the Duke of Bedford's extreme œconomy is, it seems, entirely without foundation. Though not very prodigal abroad, in his own family at least he is regular and magnificent. He pays his debts, abhors a beggar, and makes a handsome provision for his son. His

charity

charity has improved upon the proverb, and ended where it began. Admitting the whole force of this single instance of his domestic generosity (wonderful indeed, considering the narrowness of his fortune, and the little merit of his only son) the public may still perhaps be dissatisfied, and demand some other less equivocal proofs of his munificence. Sir William Draper should have entered boldly into the detail—of indigence relieved—of arts encouraged—of science patronized; men of learning protected, and works of genius rewarded;—in short, had there been a single instance, besides Mr. Rigby *, of blushing merit brought forward by the duke, for the service of the public, it should not have been omitted †.

I wish it were possible to establish my inference with the same certainty, on which I believe the principle is founded. My conclusion however was not drawn from the principle alone. I am not so unjust as to reason from one crime to another; though I think, that, of all the vices, avarice is most apt to taint and corrupt the heart. I combined the known temper of the man with

* This gentleman is supposed not to have any idea of *blushing.*

† This paragraph produced the letter from Frances, which follows this.

the

the extravagant conceffions made by the ambaffador; and though I doubt not fufficient care was taken to leave no document of any treafonable negociation, I ftill maintain that the conduct * of this minifter carries with it an internal and convincing evidence againft him. Sir William Draper feems not to know the value or force of fuch a proof. He will not permit us to judge of the motives of men, by the manifeft tendency of their actions, nor by the notorious character of their minds. He calls for papers and witneffes, with a triumphant fecurity, as if nothing could be true, but what could be proved in a court of juftice. Yet a religious man might have remembered, upon what foundation fome truths, moft interefting to mankind, have been received and eftablifhed. If it were not for the internal evidence, which the pureft of religions carries with it, what would have become of his once well-quoted decalogue, and of the meeknefs of his Chriftianity?

THE generous warmth of his refentment makes him confound the order of events. He forgets that the infults and diftreffes which the Duke of Bedford has fuffered, and which

---

* If Sir William Draper will take the trouble of looking into Torcy's Memoirs, he will fee with what little ceremony a bribe may be offered to a Duke, and with what little ceremony it was *only not accepted*.

Sir

Sir William has lamented with many delicate touches of the true pathetic, were only recorded in my letter to his Grace, not occasioned by it. It was a simple, candid narrative of facts; though, for aught I know, it may carry with it something prophetic. His Grace undoubtedly has received several ominous hints; and I think, in certain circumstances, a wise man would do well to prepare himself for the event.

But I have a charge of a heavier nature against Sir William Draper. He tells us that the Duke of Bedford is amenable to justice;—that parliament is a high and solemn tribunal; and that, if guilty, he may be punished by due course of law; and all this, he says, with as much gravity as if he believed one word of the matter. I hope indeed, the day of impeachments will arrive, before this nobleman escapes out of life;—but to refer us to that mode of proceeding now, with such a ministry, and such a house of commons as the present, what is it, but an indecent mockery of the common sense of the nation? I think he might have contented himself with defending the greatest enemy, without insulting the distresses of his country.

His concluding declaration of his opinion, with respect to the present condition of affairs, is too loose and undetermined to be of any service to the public. How strange is it that this gentleman should dedicate so much time and argument to the defence of worthless or indifferent characters, while he gives but seven solitary lines to the only subject, which can deserve his attention, or do credit to his abilities.

JUNIUS.

LETTER XLI.

TO THE PRINTER OF THE PUBLIC ADVERTISER.

SIR, 14 *Oct*, 1769.

PERFECTLY convinced as I am of my own inability to enter the lists, or use my pen, against the tow-edged sword that glitters in the hand of *Junius*, nothing but my being impelled by that uncommon kind of gratitude, which makes us not only thankful for benefits received, but inclines us to love and respect our benefactor, could tempt me forth to so unequal a combat, or prevail on me to offer even a fact to the public, through such a channel as our newspapers.

LET

Let my motive then plead my excuse, while I reply to the charge which appears most difficult to be cleared, because it is most general, which Junius has made against the Duke of Bedford.

Junius calls upon Sir William Draper to " enter boldly into the detail of indigence relieved; of arts encouraged; of science patronized; men of learning protected; and the works of genius rewarded."

Under any of these denominations, it must be extremely painful to a woman, whose highest merit should be modesty, and of course a *blushing merit*, to appear; yet truth and gratitude ought to surmount female delicacy so far, as to relate a matter of fact, which she hopes will be one proof of the injustice of the charge here quoted against the Duke of Bedford.

When his Grace was Lord Lieutenant of Ireland, the series of letters between Henry and Frances happened to fall into his hands. In the preface, Henry speaks of the distresses of his fortune, and the justifiable means by which those distresses were occasioned.—His Grace's humanity was affected; he enquired into the author's situation, and on finding it to be what is there described, unsolicited by aught but his own noble nature, he sent for Henry, and, in the most obliging and gracious manner, presented him with a patent employment which was at that time vacant.

SURE I am, that many parallel, perhaps more meritorious, instances of his Grace's munificence, might be recounted, if those, who like me, have partaken of them, had virtue sufficient to acknowledge themselves *obliged*, when they had received an *obligation*.

FRANCES.

LETTER XLII.

TO THE PRINTER OF THE PUBLIC ADVERTISER.

SIR,   20 *October*, 1769.

I VERY sincerely applaud the spirit with which a lady has paid the debt of gratitude to her benefactor. Though I think she has mistaken the point, she shews a virtue which makes her respectable. The question turned upon the personal generosity or avarice of a man, whose private fortune is immense. The proofs of his munificence must be drawn from the uses, to which he has applied that fortune. I was not speaking of a Lord Lieute-

nant

nant of Ireland, but of a rich English duke, whose wealth gave him the means of doing as much good in this country, as he derived from his power in another. I am far from wishing to lessen the merit of this single benevolent action;—perhaps it is the more conspicuous from standing alone. All I mean to say is, that it proves nothing in the present argument.

JUNIUS.

LETTER XLIII.

TO THE PRINTER OF THE PUBLIC ADVERTISER.

SIR,   19 *October*, 1769.

I AM well assured that *Junius* will never descend to a dispute with such a writer as *Modestus* (whose letter appeared in the Gazetteer of Monday) especially as the dispute must be chiefly about words. Notwithstanding the partiality of the public, it does not appear that *Junius* values himself upon any superior skill in composition, and I hope his time will always be more usefully employed than in trifling refinements of verbal criticism. *Modestus*, however, shall have no reason to triumph in the silence and moderation of *Junius*. If he knew as much of the propriety of language, as I believe he does of the facts in question, he would have been as cautious of attacking *Junius* upon his composition, as he seems to be of entering into the subject of it; yet after all, the last is the only article of any importance to the public.

I Do not wonder at the unremitted rancour with which the Duke of Bedford and his adherents invariably speak of a nation, which we well know has been too much injured to be easily forgiven. But why must *Junius* be an Irishman?—*The absurdity of his writings betrays him.*—Waving all consideration of the insult offered by *Modestus* to the declared judgment of the people (they may well bear this among the rest) let us follow the several instances, and try whether the charge be fairly supported.

First then,—the leaving a man to enjoy such repose as he can find upon a bed of torture, is severe indeed; perhaps too much so, when applied to such a trifler as Sir William Draper; but there is nothing absurd either in the idea or expression. *Modestus* cannot distinguish between a sarcasm and a contradiction.

2. I AFFIRM with *Junius*, that it is the *frequency* of the fact, which alone can make us comprehend how a man can be his own enemy. We should never arrive at the complex idea conveyed by these words, if we had only seen one or two instances of a man acting to his own prejudice. Offer the proposition to a child, or a man unused to compound his ideas, and you will soon see how little either of them understand you. It is not a simple idea arising from a single fact, but a very complex idea arising from many facts well observed, and accurately compared.

3. MODESTUS could not, without great affectation, mistake the meaning of *Junius*, when he speaks of a man who is the bitterest enemy of his friends. He could not but know, that *Junius* spoke, not of a false or hollow friendship, but of a real intention to serve, and that intention producing the worst effects of enmity. Whether the description be strictly applicable to Sir William Draper is another question. *Junius* does not say that it is more *criminal* for a man to be the enemy of his friends than his own, though he might have affirmed it with truth. In a moral light a man may certainly take greater liberties with himself than with another. To sacrifice ourselves merely is a weakness we may indulge in, if we think proper, for we do it at our own hazard

hazard and expence; but, under the pretence of friendship, to sport with the reputation, or sacrifice the honour of another, is something worse than weakness; and if, in favour of the foolish intention, we do not call it a crime, we must allow at least that it arises from an overweening, busy, meddling impudence.—*Junius* says only, and he says truly, that it is more extraordinary, that it involves a greater contradiction than the other; and is it not a maxim received in life, that in general we can determine more wisely for others than for ourselves? The reason of it is so clear in argument, that it hardly wants the confirmation of experience. Sir William Draper, I confess, is an exception to the general rule, though not much to his credit.

4. If this gentleman will go back to his Ethicks, he may perhaps discover the truth of what *Junius* says, *that no outward tyranny can reach the mind.* The tortures of the body may be introduced by way of ornament or illustration to represent those of the mind, but strictly there is no similitude between them. They are totally different both in their cause and operation. The wretch, who suffers upon the rack, is merely passive; but when the mind is tortured, it is not at the command of any outward power. It is the sense of guilt which constitutes the punishment, and creates

that

that torture with which the guilty mind acts upon itself.

5. He misquotes what *Junius* says of conscience, and makes the sentence ridiculous, by making it his own.

So much for composition. Now for fact.—*Junius* it seems has mistaken the duke of Bedford. His Grace had all the proper feelings of a father, though he took care to suppress the appearance of them. Yet it was an occasion, one would think, on which he need not have been ashamed of his grief;—on which less fortitude would have done him more honour. I can conceive indeed a benevolent motive for his endeavouring to assume an air of tranquillity in his own family, and I wish I could discover any thing, in the rest of his character, to justify my assigning that motive to his behaviour. But is there no medium? Was it necessary to appear abroad, to ballot at the India-house, and make a public display, tho' it were only of an apparent insensibility?—I know we are treading on tender ground, and *Junius*, I am convinced, does not wish to urge this question farther. Let the friends of the Duke of Bedford observe that humble silence, which becomes their situation. They should recollect that there are still some facts

facts * in store, at which human nature would shudder. I shall be understood by those whom it concerns, when I say that these facts go farther † than to the Duke.

It is not inconsistent to suppose that a man may be quite indifferent about one part of a charge, yet severely stung with another, and though he feels no remorse, that he may wish to be revenged. The charge of insensibility carries a reproach indeed, but no danger with it.—*Junius* had said, *there are others who would assassinate*. *Modestus*, knowing his man, will not suffer the insinuation to be divided, but fixes it all upon the Duke of Bedford.

Without determining upon what evidence *Junius* would *choose to be condemned*, I will venture to maintain, in opposition to *Modestus*, or to Mr. Rigby (who is certainly not

---

* The Duke had an inventory taken of the Marquis's clothes, sold them all, and pocketed the money: but the Marchioness gave her late husband's servant the value of them out of her own pocket.

† When the incomparable Marchioness died, the Duchess of Bedford, her mother in law, had all her wearing apparel sold, and put the money in her pocket. In a fortnight after the unfortunate death of the Marquis, his mother the Duchess had a route at Bedford House.

Modestus)

Modestus) or any other of the Bloomsbury gang, that the evidence against the Duke of Bedford is as strong as any presumptive evidence can be. It depends upon a combination of facts and reasoning, which require no confirmation from the anecdote of the Duke of Marlborough. This anecdote was referred to merely to shew how ready a great man may be to receive a great bribe; and if *Modestus* could read the original, he would see that the expression, *only not accepted*, was probably the only one in our language that exactly fitted the case. The bribe, offered to the Duke of Marlborough, was not refused..

I cannot conclude without taking notice of this honest gentleman's learning, and wishing he had given us a little more of it. When he accidentally found himself so near speaking truth, it was rather unfair of him to leave out the *non potuisse refelli*. As it stands, the *pudet hæc opprobria* may be divided equally between Mr. Rigby and the Duke of Bedford. Mr. Rigby, I take for granted, will assert his natural right to the modesty of the quotation, and leave all the opprobrium to his Grace..

PHILO JUNIUS.

LETTER XLIV.

TO THE PRINTER OF THE PUBLIC AD-
VERTISER.

SIR,   27 *October*, 1769.

IT is not wonderful that the great cause, in which this country is engaged, should have roused and engrossed the whole attention of the people. I rather admire the generous spirit, with which they feel and assert their interest in this important question, than blame them for their indifference about any other. When the constitution is openly invaded, when the first original right of the people, from which all laws derive their authority, is directly attacked, inferior grievances naturally lose their force, and are suffered to pass by without punishment or observation. The present ministry are as singularly marked by their fortune, as by their crimes. Instead of atoning for their former conduct by any wise or popular measure, they have found, in the enormity of one fact, a cover and defence for a series of measures, which must have been fatal to any other administration. I fear we are too remiss in observing the whole of their proceedings.

ings. Struck with the principal figure, we do not sufficiently mark in what manner the canvafs is filled up. Yet furely it is not a lefs crime, nor lefs fatal in its confequences, to encourage a flagrant breach of the law by a military force, than to make ufe of the forms of parliament to deftroy the conftitution.—The miniftry feem determined to give us a choice of difficulties, and, if poffible, to perplex us with the multitude of their offences. The expedient is worthy of the Duke of Grafton. But though he has preferved a gradation and variety in his meafures, we fhould remember that the principle is uniform. Dictated by the fame fpirit, they deferve the fame attention. The following fact, though of the moft alarming nature, has not yet been clearly ftated to the public, nor have the confequences of it been fufficiently underftood. Had I taken it up at an earlier period, I fhould have been accufed of an uncandid, malignant precipitation, as if I watched for an unfair advantage againft the miniftry, and would not allow them a reafonable time to do their duty. They now ftand without excufe. Inftead of employing the leifure they have had, in a ftrict examination of the offence, and punifhing the offenders, they feem to have confidered *that* indulgence as a fecurity to them, that, with a little time and management, the whole affair might be buried in silence, and utterly forgotten.

A Major General of the army * is arrested by the sheriff's officers for a considerable debt. He

---

* MAJOR GENERAL WILLIAM GANSELL, of the 55th regiment. He was a great connoisseur, particularly in paintings, of which he had a very large and valuable collection; he also possessed a very considerable estate, besides the emoluments he derived from his profession; but his passion for paintings greatly embarrassed his circumstances. He was nephew to the celebrated Dr. Ward, who, at his death, December 1761, left him all the money he owed him by bond or otherwise, any three of his pictures the General should choose, and one thousand pounds in money.

SATURDAY, May 21st, 1770, the following order came out to the brigade of guards. Parole Hounslow.

B. O. His Majesty has signified to the field officer in waiting, that he has been acquainted that Serjeant Bacon of the first regiment; and Serjeant Parke of the Coldstream regiment; William Powell, William Hart, James Potter, and Joseph Collins, private soldiers in the first regiment of foot guards, were more or less concerned in the rescue of Major General Gansell, in September last; the King hopes, and is willing to believe, they did not know the Major General was arrested, and only thought they were delivering an officer in distress; however his Majesty commands, that they should be severely reprimanded for acting in this business as they have done; and strictly orders for the future, that no non commissioned officer or soldier do presume to interfere

He perſuades them to conduct him to the
Tilt-yard in St. James's Park, under ſome
pretence of buſineſs, which it imported him
to ſettle before he was confined. He applies
to a ſerjeant, not immediately on duty, to
assist

fere with bailiffs, or arreſts, on any account or pretence whatſoever, the crime being of a very atrocious
nature; and if any are found guilty of diſobeying this
order, they will be moſt ſeverely puniſhed. This order
to be read immediately at the head of every company in
the brigade of guards, that no man may plead ignorance for the future.

THE General ſtill continuing involved in debt, five
bailiffs, two Hydes, Felthouſe, Sly, and Reeves, at the
ſuit of Samuel Lee, a ſurgeon, went on the 26th of
Auguſt 1773, to arreſt him at his apartments in Craven
Street, for the ſum of of 134l. The General made re-
ſiſtance on being attacked in his own apartments, by
firing two piſtols through the door, but the bailiffs broke
in upon him, and carried him off. On the 14th of September, the General was tried at the Old Bailey for his
life for firing the piſtols. The bailiffs ſwore what they
thought neceſſary to convict him. But Mr. Juſtice
Nares obſerved, that conſidering the evidence of the two
Hydes and Felthouſe by itſelf, without at all looking to
what the evidences for the General had ſworn, it was altogether improbable and contradictory, and pointed out
parts of it which could not poſſibly be believed. The
Jury were of the Judge's opinion, and immediately
brought in a verdict of Not Guilty, without going out of
Court. The General in his defence mentioned that he
had read in Blackſtone's Commentaries, that an Eng-
liſhman's

assist with some of his companions in favouring his escape. He attempts it. A bustle ensues. The bailiffs claim their prisoner. † An officer of the guards, not then on duty, takes part in the affair, applies to the ‡ lieutenant commanding the Tilt-yard guard, and urges him to turn out his guard to relieve a general officer. The lieutenant declines interfering in person, but stands at a distance, and suffers the business to be done. The officer takes upon himself to order out the guard. In a moment they are in arms, quit their guard, march, rescue the general, and drive away the sheriffs officers, who, in vain represent their right to the prisoner, and the nature of the arrest. The soldiers first conduct the general into the guard-room, then escort him to a place of safety, with bayonets fixed, and in all the forms of military

lishman's house was his castle, and that he had lived in the apartments in which he was attacked thirty-eight years. He was however detained upon the arrest, and committed to the Fleet Prison, where he died suddenly on the 28th of July 1774. He was a very stout man, but corpulent; his death was imputed to the bursting of a blood vessel.

† Lieutenant Dodd.

‡ Lieutenant Garth, now a Brigadier General in the West Indies, and an excellent officer.

triumph

triumph. I will not enlarge upon the various circumstances which attended this atrocious proceeding. The personal injury received by the officers of the law in the execution of their duty, may perhaps be atoned for by some private compensation. I consider nothing but the wound, which has been given to the law itself, to which no remedy has been applied, no satisfaction made. Neither is it my design to dwell upon the misconduct of the parties concerned, any farther than is necessary to shew the behaviour of the ministry in its true light. I would make every compassionate allowance for the infatuation of the prisoner, the false and criminal discretion of one officer, and the madness of another. I would leave the ignorant soldiers entirely out of the question. They are certainly the least guilty, though they are the only persons who have yet suffered, even in the appearance of punishment.† The fact itself, however atrocious, is not the principal point to be considered. It might have happened under a more regular government, and with guards better disciplined than ours. The main question is, in what manner have the ministry acted on this extraordinary occasion. A general officer calls upon the king's own guard, then actually on

† SOME of them were confined.

duty,

duty, to rescue him from the laws of his country; yet in this moment he is in a situation no worse, than if he had not committed an offence, equally enormous in a civil and military view.—A lieutenant upon duty designedly quits his guard, and suffers it to be drawn out by another officer, for a purpose, which he well knew (as we may collect from an appearance of caution, which only makes his behaviour the more criminal) to be in the highest degree illegal. Has this gentleman been called to a court martial to answer for his conduct? No. Has it been censured? No. Has it been in any shape enquired into? No.—Another lieutenant, not upon duty, nor even in his regimentals, is daring enough to order out the king's guard, over which he had properly no command, and engages them in a violation of the laws of his country, perhaps the most singular and extravagant that ever was attempted— What punishment has *he* suffered? Literally none. Supposing he should be prosecuted at common law for the rescue, will that circumstance, from which the ministry can derive no merit, excuse or justify their suffering so flagrant a breach of military discipline to pass by unpunished, and unnoticed? Are they aware of the outrage offered to their sovereign, when his own proper guard is ordered out to stop by main force the execution

tion of his laws? What are we to conclude from so scandalous a neglect of their duty, but that they have other views, which can only be answered by securing the attachment of the guards? The minister would hardly be so cautious of offending them, if he did not mean, in due time, to call for their assistance.

With respect to the parties themselves, let it be observed, that these gentlemen are neither young officers, nor very young men. Had they belonged to the unfledged race of ensigns, who infest our streets, and dishonour our public places, it might perhaps be sufficient to send them back to that discipline, from which their parents, judging lightly from the maturity of their vices, had removed them too soon. In this case, I am sorry to see, not so much the folly of youth, as the spirit of the corps, and the connivance of government. I do not question that there are many brave and worthy officers in the regiments of guards. But considering them as a corps, I fear, it will be found that they are neither good soldiers, nor good subjects. Far be it from me to insinuate the most distant reflection upon the army. On the contrary, I honour and esteem the profession; and if these gentlemen were better soldiers, I am sure they would be better subjects. It

is

is not that there is any internal vice or defect in the profession itself, as regulated in this country, but that it is the spirit of this particular corps, to despise their profession, and that while they vainly assume the lead of the army, they make it matter of impertinent comparison, and triumph over the bravest troops in the world (I mean our marching regiments) that *they* indeed stand, upon higher ground, and are privileged to neglect the laborious forms of military discipline and duty. Without dwelling longer upon a most invidious subject, I shall leave it to military men, who have seen a service more active than the parade, to determine whether or no I speak truth.

How far this dangerous spirit has been encouraged by government, and to what pernicious purposes it may be applied hereafter, well deserves our most serious consideration. I know indeed, that when this affair happened, an affectation of alarm ran through the ministry. Something must be done to save appearances. The case was too flagrant to be passed by absolutely without notice. But how have they acted? Instead of ordering the officers concerned, (and who, strictly speaking, are alone guilty) to be put under arrest, and brought to trial, they would have it understood, that they did their duty completely, in

con-

confining a serjeant and four private soldiers, until they should be demanded by the civil power; so that while the officers, who ordered or permitted the thing to be done, escape without censure, the poor men who obeyed those orders, who in a military view are no way responsible for what they did, and who for that reason have been discharged by the civil magistrates, are the only objects whom the ministry have thought proper to expose to punishment. They did not venture to bring even these men to a court martial, because they knew their evidence would be fatal to some persons, whom they were determined to protect. Otherwise, I doubt not, the lives of these unhappy, friendless soldiers, would long since have been sacrificed without scruple, to the security of their guilty officers.

I have been accused of endeavouring to enflame the passions of the people.—Let me now appeal to their understanding. If there be any tool of administration daring enough, to deny these facts, or shameless enough to defend the conduct of the ministry, let him come forward. I care not under what title he appears. He shall find me ready to maintain the truth of my narrative, and the justice of my observations upon it, at the hazard of my utmost credit with the public.

Under the most arbitrary governments, the common administration of justice is suffered to take its course. The subject, though robbed of his share in the legislature, is still protected by the laws. The political freedom of the English constitution was once the pride and honour of an Englishman. The civil equality of the laws preserved the property, and defended the safety of the subject. Are these glorious privileges the birthright of the people, or are we only tenants at the will of the ministry?—But that I know there is a spirit of resistance in the hearts of my countrymen, that they value life, not by its conveniencies, but by the independence and dignity of their condition, I should, at this moment, appeal only to their discretion. I should persuade them to banish from their minds all memory of what we were; I should tell them this is not a time to remember that we were Englishmen; and give it as my last advice, to make some early agreement with the minister, that since it has pleased him to rob us of those political rights, which once distinguished the inhabitants of a country, where honour was happiness, he would leave us at least the humble, obedient security of citizens, and graciously condescend to protect us in our submission.

JUNIUS.

LETTER

LETTER XLV.

TO THE PRINTER OF THE PUBLIC ADVERTISER.

SIR, *November 14, 1769.*

THE variety of remarks which have been made upon the laſt letter of *Junius*, and my own opinion of the writer, who, whatever may be his faults, is certainly not a weak man, have induced me to examine, with ſome attention, the ſubject of that letter. I could not perſuade myſelf that, while he had plenty of important materials, he would have taken up a light or trifling occaſion to attack the miniſtry; much leſs could I conceive that it was his intention to ruin the officers concerned in the reſcue of General Ganſell, or to injure the General himſelf. Theſe are little objects, and can no way contribute to the great purpoſes he ſeems to have in view by addreſſing himſelf to the public.——Without conſidering the ornamented ſtile he has adopted, I determined to look farther into the matter, before I decided upon the merits of his letter. The firſt ſtep I took was to enquire into the truth of the facts; for if theſe were either falſe or miſre-

misrepresented, the most artful exertion of his understanding, in reasoning upon them, would only be a disgrace to him.—Now, Sir, I have found every circumstance stated by *Junius* to be literally true. General Gansell persuaded the bailiffs to conduct him to the parade, and certainly solicited a corporal and other soldiers to assist him in making his escape. Captain Dodd * did certainly apply to Captain Garth for the assistance of his guard. Captain Garth declined appearing himself, but stood aloof, while the other took upon him to order out the King's guard, and by main force rescued the General. It is also strictly true, that the General was escorted by a file of musqueteers to a place of security. —These are facts, Mr. Woodfall, which I promise you no gentleman in the guards will deny. If all or any of them are false, why are they not contradicted by the parties themselves? However secure against military censure, they have yet a character to lose, and surely, if they are innocent, it is not beneath them to pay some attention to the opinion of the public.

THE force of *Junius*'s Observations upon these facts cannot be better marked, than by

---

* Dodd and Garth, though only lieutenants, had captains rank. All the lieutenants of the Guards have captains rank.

stating

stating and refuting the objections which have been made to them. One writer says, "Admitting the officers have offended, they are punishable at common law, and will you have a British subject punished twice for the same offence?"—I answer that they have committed two offences, both very enormous, and violated two laws. The rescue is one offence, the flagrant breach of discipline another, and hitherto it does not appear that they have been punished, or even censured for either. Another gentleman lays much stress upon the calamity of the case, and instead of disproving facts, appeals at once to the compassion of the public. This idea, as well as the insinuation, that *depriving the parties of their commissions would be an injury to their creditors*, can only refer to General Gansell. The other officers are in no distress, therefore have no claim to compassion, nor does it appear, that their creditors, if they have any, are more likely to be satisfied by their continuing in the guards. But this sort of plea will not hold in any shape. Compassion to an offender, who has grossly violated the laws, is in effect a cruelty to the peaceable subject who has observed them; and, even admitting the force of any alleviating circumstances, it is nevertheless true, that, in this instance, the royal compassion has interposed too soon. The legal and proper

per mercy of a King of England may remit the punishment, but ought not to stop the trial.

BESIDES these particular objections, there has been a cry raised against *Junius* for his malice and injustice in attacking the ministry upon an event, which they could neither hinder nor foresee. This, I must affirm, is a false representation of his argument. He lays no stress upon the event itself, as a ground of accusation against the ministry, but dwells entirely upon their subsequent conduct. He does not say that they are answerable for the offence, but for the scandalous neglect of their duty, in suffering an offence, so flagrant, to pass by without notice or inquiry. Supposing them ever so regardless of what they owe to the public, and as indifferent about the opinion as they are about the interests of their country, what answer, as officers of the crown, will they give to *Junius,* when he asks them, *Are they aware of the outrage offered to their Sovereign, when his own proper guard is ordered out to stop, by main force, the execution of his laws?*—And when we see a ministry giving such a strange unaccountable protection to the officers of the guards, is it unfair to suspect, that they have some secret and unwarrantable motives for their conduct? If they feel themselves injured

jured by such a suspicion, why do they not immediately clear themselves from it, by doing their duty? For the honour of the guards, I cannot help expressing another suspicion, that if the commanding officer had not received a secret injunction to the contrary, he would, in the ordinary course of his business, have applied for a court martial to try the two subalterns; the one for quitting his guard—the other for taking upon him the command of the guard, and employing it in the manner he did. I do not mean to enter into or defend the severity, with which *Junius* treats the guards. On the contrary, I will suppose for a moment, that they deserve a very different character. If this be true, in what light will they consider the conduct of the two subalterns, but as a general reproach and disgrace to the whole corps? And will they not wish to see them censured in a military way, if it were only for the credit and discipline of the regiment.

Upon the whole, Sir, the Ministry seem to me to have taken a very improper advantage of the good-nature of the public, whose humanity, they found, considered nothing in this affair but the distress of General Gansell. They would persuade us that it was only a common rescue by a few disorderly soldiers, and not the formal deliberate act of the king's guard, headed by an officer, and the public has fallen into the deception. I think, therefore, we are obliged to *Junius* for the care he has taken to enquire into the facts, and for the just commentary with which he has given them to the world.—For my own part, I am as unwilling as any man to load the unfortunate; but, really, Sir, the precedent, with respect to the guards, is of a most important nature, and alarming enough (considering the consequences with which it may be attended) to deserve a parliamentary enquiry: when the guards are daring enough, not only to violate their own discipline, but publicly and with the most atrocious violence to stop the execution of the laws, and when such extraordinary offences pass with impunity, believe me, Sir, the precedent strikes deep.

PHILO JUNIUS.

LETTER

LETTER XLVI.

TO JUNIUS.

SIR,

YOU challenge any tool of administration to defend the conduct of ministry. I accept of your challenge, though it is not addressed to me. I am no tool of administration, but your equal, Junius, perhaps your superior in every thing that may become a man. I desire, for judges of the contest, justice, candour, and impartiality—I dare you to your uttermost, and if I do not make you appear in the eyes of all reasonable men, as contemptible as you deserve to be, let the scorn be transferred to myself.

You say you will defend the truth of your narrative, and the justice of your observations, at the risk of your "*utmost credit.*" The risk is small, but it is all you have, and therefore I take you at your word. Facts that come from Junius are liable to suspicion; but here he is supported by public fame. All the facts in your tedious narrative I have heard before; and the only new information you have given the public is, that one of the officers engaged in this affair was not in regimentals. But though I have heard all, and am probably inclined to believe that the greatest part is true, I would not be understood to vouch for any. On the other hand, I will not imitate you, and assert when I cannot prove.; let the fact therefore be thrown out of dispute, till it is better ascertained, and let the justice of your observations be my present subject.

You accuse the minister of a crime, in relation to the arrest of a general officer: I ask you what that crime is? Had he screened and protected an officer of the highest rank from justice, I could have understood you, and the case would have been truly alarming; but were you to say so, the falsehood would be confuted by the personal knowledge of all men. Tender of the regular execution of justice, the minister interposed beyond his province in support of it; I say, beyond his province; and had your judgment been equal to your malice, you would have accused him of interfering in the execution of the law, without being required by the civil power. You do not see where you attempt to lead a deluded people. If you had known the constitution, if you seriously meant it well, you never would have made it a crime in the minister

nister that he did not do more; you might, with some appearance, have blamed him for interposing at all.

YET even then, his crime would have been a zeal, perhaps an officious zeal, to secure criminals, who, by their low rank and situation, might be naturally suspected of a design to withdraw themselves from justice. But you say this was only to save appearances; and your proof is, that the officers were not secured. The officers were not secured, because there was no fear of their running away. They are still open to a prosecution; and if the spirit of the times is such, that no indulgence can be given for an offence so common, and generally considered as a venial one, let the utmost severity of the law be exerted against them; and I could wish it were exerted against many other greater offenders.

IT would, perhaps, be unjust to accuse you of enforcing the enormity of the crime from enmity to the criminals. I am certain it would be ridiculous to suppose you enforced it from respect to the laws. But a minister was to be wounded; and provided this could be done, no matter through whose side the weapon struck. I do not dwell on the barbarity of attempting to load the unfortunate. You tell a generous nation, that the principal person

person concerned is in no worse situation than if he had not committed the offence; but you take care to lead its attention from what his situation is. You dare not venture to expose to the compassion of a generous nation, a man of some rank, ruined, and in prison; and you present no objects but such as are calculated to inflame; when humanity should have prompted you to present the most proper to extenuate.

We know what the common law decrees in offences of this nature; and it requires not the help of Junius to execute its decrees. But he says the offenders should be punished also by military law. Perhaps, in rigour, they should: but are we only to listen to the voice of severity? And is Junius the man who bids us shut our ears to indulgence? Where was his zeal for the law when the peace of this capital was disturbed by a lawless mob? And why did not Junius arraign the conduct of a minister, whose lenity overlooked the most gross insult that ever was offered to order? When the king was, in a manner, besieged in his palace, a compassionate respect for the delusion of a multitude withheld that exertion of power which the law authorised. Did Junius then stand forth the champion of his outraged sovereign? No, he dignified the insult with an honourable name, and branded

branded the moderation of government with a name of infamy. But let two inconsiderable officers, from inconsiderate regard to one of superior rank, assist him to escape from a bailiff, and Junius is immediately in arms. The constitution is already ruined, and private property is no longer secure. What if the king only delays that military punishment, which you are so anxious to have inflicted, only to secure the creditors payment? If these people are broke, the debt is lost. But were the king and his ministers to act with the purity and the wisdom of angels, your heart would find something amiss, and your paultry interest of a day would compel you to utter your censure.

BLINDNESS herself must see through the purpose of the invidious comparison you draw between the guards and the marching regiments. *Divide et impera*, is a maxim you understand: but happily for this nation, you are but a bungler in the application of it. The guards despise your malicious invectives, as the rest of the army do your insidious encomiums. You say, the minister is tender of the guards, because, in due time, he will make use of them. I hope, if the constitution is attacked, not only they, but every good subject in the kingdom will stand up in its defence. But you will not succeed in your design to make your party begin that attack, by perfuading them that force may be firft employed againft themfelves. The experienced lenity of government is proof againft your fedition, and though your defperation would involve *all* in ruin, you will not find a *part* difpofed to fupport you.

To conclude: your letter is a dull invective. The ftory you tell has neither the charm of novelty, or fpirit to recommend it. The confequences you draw from an incident, which you admit to be a very common one, are as abfurd as they are malicious. And in your preface and peroration, you refemble thofe termagent women, who, whilft they are tearing out the eyes of a hufband who does not defend himfelf, never ceafe the cry of murder.

MODESTUS.

LETTER XLVII.

TO JUNIUS.

SIR,

THREE weeks are elapsed since you favoured the public with an essay on the arrest of a general officer. You wrested the circumstances with which it was attended, into a crime against administration. You told the story in your own way; you reasoned upon it in your own way also; you abused, you praised, you challenged, and you concluded. In all this, it would be difficult to decide, whether the inveteracy of your malice, the absurdity of your argument, the barbarity of your intention, or the dulness of your stile and composition, appeared most conspicuous.

But, Sir, waving the rest, you challenged, and these are the precise terms of your defiance: 'I have been accused of endeavouring to inflame the passions of the people, &c.'

Two days after your letter made its appearance in the Public Advertiser, an answer to it appeared in the Gazetteer, in which

your challenge was accepted in the following words: 'You challenge any tool of admi-
'niftration to defend the conduct of the mi-
'niftry; I accept of your challenge, though
'it is not addreſſed to me. I am no tool of
'adminiftration, but your equal, Junius,
'perhaps your fuperior, in every thing that
'may become a man. I defire for judges
'of the conteft, juftice, candour, and impar-
'tiality. I dare you to the uttermoft; and
'if I do not make you appear, in the eyes of
'all reaſonable men, as contemptible as you
'deſerve to be, let the ſcorn be transferred
'to myſelf.'

WHAT is the reafon, Junius, that you have hitherto taken no notice of that letter? The author of it, too candid to affirm what he could not immediately prove, fuppoſed, in his argument, your narrative to be true; and even on that fuppofition, he demonftrated your obfervations not only unjuft, but in-
confiftent, even to abfurdity. But if he could not with certain knowledge deny the fact, he doubted it; he told you fo; and in the belief that no man would give a formal chal-
lange without purfuing it, he has enquired into the truth of that fact. He tells you now, and will maintain it at the utmoſt hazard of *his* credit with the public, that your narrative is no leſs falſe than your obfervations are fallacious.

lacious. It is false (for instance) that the general officer applied to a serjeant, not on duty, to favour his escape. It is false, that the officer of the guard stood at a distance, and suffered the business to be done. He was spoken to by the other officer in the coffee-house, and he not only declined interfering in person, but flatly refused his assistance directly or indirectly. He did more: he dissuaded his brother officer from his intention, and believed he had prevailed. His only fault was, being the dupe of the other's apparent repentance, who left the coffee-house, as if he intended to proceed no farther in the attempt; and took the opportunity to apply to some soldiers of the guard, while the officer who commanded it remained at the coffee-house. It is false that the guard was turned out, or under arms. And it is a most malicious construction of the fairest conduct, to blame administration, because these gentlemen have not been punished by military law.

The truth is, that it was proposed to try the offenders by military law, immediately after the offence was committed; but, in a consultation with the civil magistrate, it was judged improper, lest a military trial should prejudge the action now depending, and in which the offenders are at present under bail.

A fair

A fair trial is the right of every Englishman, whatever offence he may be guilty of. Our civil rights are our most precious blessings; and our form of trial is the bulwark of these rights; and, Sir, you contradict the principles you profess, when you endeavour to set up martial, in opposition to common law, and give that the lead which ought to follow. Had these gentlemen been first tried by military law, the evidences brought before a court martial must have been afterwards examined in the courts of law; but witnesses already examined upon oath, according to the arbitrary proceedings of a court martial, cannot be unexceptionable in a subsequent civil action. Their evidence, however extorted, would awe them to conceal, or disguise the truth, which our form of civil trial is so well calculated to discover. And you, Junius, a patriot, and an assertor of the rights of Englishmen, would have declaimed and exclaimed, with some appearance of justice, against the proceedings of a court martial, which should have deprived these officers of that fair and legal trial which they have a right, as Englishmen, to demand.

Our military laws prescribe the punishment of cashiering for offences of this nature. But how is this crime to be proved? Only by the verdict of a jury in a civil action;

tion; and the judgment upon it is evidence of record in the subsequent court martial: but these are matters of which you are ignorant. You go on in your old method, to clap the cart before the horse; and you would have punished by military law, an offence which military law cannot take cognizance of, until it has been legally found one by the verdict of a jury. Thus, blinded by your passion, or unacquainted with the constitution, you would overturn it, to wreck your resentment against a ministry, which, in this instance at least, has acted in its truest spirit.

It is time, Junius, you should think of the challenge you gave. I know you to be slow, and I have not hurried you.

MODESTUS.

LETTER

LETTER XLVIII.

TO THE PRINTER OF THE PUBLIC ADVERTISER.

SIR, 15 *Nov.* 1769.

I ADMIT the claim of a gentleman, who publishes in the Gazetteer under the name of *Modestus*. He has some right to expect an answer from me; though, I think, not so much from the merit or importance of his objections, as from my own voluntary engagement. I had a reason for not taking notice of him sooner, which, as he is a candid person, I believe he will think sufficient. In my first letter, I took for granted, from the time which had elapsed, that there was no intention to censure, nor even to try the persons concerned in the rescue of General Gansell; but *Modestus* having since either affirmed, or strongly insinuated, that the offenders might still be brought to a legal trial, any attempt to prejudge the cause, or to prejudice the minds of a jury, or a court martial, would be highly improper.

A MAN, more hostile to the ministry than I am, would not so often remind them of their

their duty. If the Duke of Grafton will not perform the duty of his station, why is he minister?—I will not descend to a scurrilous altercation with any man: but this is a subject too important to be passed over with silent indifference. If the gentlemen, whose conduct is in question, are not brought to a trial, the Duke of Grafton shall hear from me again.

The motives on which I am supposed to have taken up this cause, are of little importance, compared with the facts themselves, and the observations I have made upon them. Without a vain profession of integrity, which, in these times might justly be suspected, I shall shew myself in effect a friend to the interests of my countrymen, and leave it to them to determine, whether I am moved by a personal malevolence to three private gentlemen, or merely by a hope of perplexing the ministry, or whether I am animated by a just and honourable purpose of obtaining a satisfaction to the laws of this country, equal, if possible, to the violation they have suffered.

JUNIUS.

LETTER

LETTER XLIX.

TO HIS GRACE THE DUKE OF GRAFTON.

MY LORD,   29 *Nov.* 1769.

THOUGH my opinion of your Grace's integrity was but little affected by the coyness with which you received Mr. Vaughan's proposals, I confess I give you some credit for your discretion. You had a fair opportunity of displaying a certain delicacy, of which you had not been suspected; and you were in the right to make use of it. By laying in a moderate stock of reputation, you undoubtedly meant to provide for the future necessities of your character, that with an honourable resistance upon record, you might safely indulge your genius, and yield to a favourite inclination with security. But you have discovered your purposes too soon; and, instead of the modest reserve of virtue, have shewn us the termagent chastity of a prude, who gratifies her passions with distinction, and prosecutes one lover for a rape, while she solicits the lewd embraces of another.

Your

Your cheek turns pale; for a guilty conscience tells you, you are undone.—Come forward, thou virtuous minister, and tell the world by what interest Mr. Hine has been recommended to so extraordinary a mark of his Majesty's favour; what was the price of the patent he has bought, and to what honourable purpose the purchase-money has been applied. Nothing less than many thousands could pay Colonel Burgoyne's expences at Preston *. Do you dare to prosecute such a creature as Vaughan, while you are basely setting up the Royal Patronage to auction? Do you dare to complain of an attack upon your own honour, while you are selling the favours of the crown, to raise a fund for corrupting the morals of the people? And, do you think it possible such enormities should escape without impeachment? It is indeed highly your interest to maintain the present house of commons. Having sold the nation to you in gross, they will undoubtedly protect you in the detail; for while they patronize your crimes, they feel for their own.

JUNIUS.

* Expences of his election there. The Colonel brought in his light dragoons to his assistance, and Preston seemed like a town taken by storm. For his behaviour at this election a suit was brought against him, and he was fined 1000l.

LETTER

LETTER L.

TO HIS GRACE THE DUKE OF GRAFTON.

MY LORD,   12 *Dec.* 1769.

I FIND with some surprise, that you are not supported as you deserve. Your most determined advocates have scruples about them, which you are unacquainted with; and, though there be nothing too hazardous for your Grace to engage in, there are some things too infamous for the vilest prostitute of a news-paper to defend. In what other manner shall we account for the profound, submissive silence, which you and your friends have observed upon a charge, which called immediately for the clearest refutation, and would have justified the severest measures of resentment? I did not attempt to blast your character by an indirect, ambiguous insinuation, but candidly stated to you a plain fact, which struck directly at the integrity of a privy counsellor, of a first commissioner of the treasury, and of a leading minister, who is supposed to enjoy the first share in his Majesty's confidence. In every one of these capacities I employed the most moderate terms to charge you with

treachery

treachery to your Sovereign, and breach of truſt in your office. I accuſed you of having ſold a patent place in the collection of the cuſtoms at Exeter, to one Mr. Hine, who, unable or unwilling to depoſit the whole purchaſe-money himſelf, raiſed part of it by contribution, and has now a certain Doctor Brooke quartered upon the ſalary for one hundred pounds a year.—No ſale by the candle was ever conducted with greater formality—I affirm that the price, at which the place was knocked down (and which, I have good reaſon to think, was not leſs than three thouſand five hundred pounds) was, with your connivance and conſent, paid to Colonel Burgoyne, to reward him, I preſume, for the decency of his deportment at Preſton; or to reimburſe him, perhaps, for the fine of one thouſand pounds, which, for that very deportment, the court of King's Bench thought proper to ſet upon him.—It is not often that the chief juſtice and the prime miniſter are ſo ſtrangely at variance in their opinions of men and things.

I thank God there is not in human nature a degree of impudence daring enough to deny the charge I have fixed upon you. Your courteous ſecretary*, your confiden-

---

* Thomas Bradshaw.

tial

tial architect † are silent as the grave. Even
Mr. Rigby's countenance fails him. He violates his second nature, and blushes whenever he speaks of you.—Perhaps the noble
Colonel himself will relieve you. No man
is more tender of his reputation. He is not
only nice, but perfectly sore in every thing
that touches his honour. If any man, for
example, were to accuse him of taking his
stand at a gaming-table, and watching, with
the soberest attention, for a fair opportunity
of engaging a drunken young nobleman at
piquet, he would undoubtedly consider it as
an infamous aspersion upon his character,
and resent it like a man of honour.—Acquitting him therefore of drawing a regular
and splendid subsistence from any unworthy
practices, either in his own house or elsewhere, let me ask your Grace, for what military merits you have been pleased to reward
him with a military government? He had a
regiment of dragoons, which one would imagine, was at least an equivalent for any services he ever performed. Besides, he is but a
young officer considering his preferment,
and, except in his activity at Preston, not very conspicuous in his profession. But it
seems, the sale of a civil employment was not

---

† Mr. Taylor and George Ross, the Scotch agent
and confidante of Lord Mansfield, are said to have
managed the business.

sus-

sufficient, and military governments, which were intended for the support of worn out veterans, must be thrown into the scale, to defray the extensive bribery of a contested election. Are these the steps you take to secure to your sovereign the attachment of his army? With what countenance dare you appear in the royal presence, branded as you are with the infamy of a notorious breach of trust? With what countenance can you take your seat at the treasury-board, or in council, when you feel that every circulating whisper is at your expence alone, and stabs you to the heart? Have you a single friend in parliament so shameless, so thoroughly abandoned, as to undertake your defence. You know, my Lord, that there is not a man in either house, whose character, however flagitious, would not be ruined by mixing his reputation with yours; and does not your heart inform you, that you are degraded below the condition of a man, when you are obliged to hear these insults with submission, and even to thank me for my moderation?

We are told, by the highest judicial authority, that Mr. Vaughan's offer to purchase the reversion of a patent in Jamaica (which he was otherwise sufficiently entitled to) amounted to a high misdemeanour. Be it so: and if he deserves it, let him be punished nifhed. But the learned judge might have had a fairer opportunity of difplaying the powers of his eloquence. Having delivered himfelf with fo much energy upon the criminal nature, and dangerous confequences of any attempt to corrupt a man in your Grace's ftation, what would he have faid to the minifter himfelf, to that very privy counfellor, to that firft commiffioner of the treafury, who does not wait for, but impatiently folicits the touch of corruption; who employs the meaneft of his creatures in thefe honourable fervices, and, forgetting the genius and fidelity of his fecretary, defcends to apply to his houfe-builder for affiftance?

This affair, my Lord, will do infinite credit to government, if, to clear your chatacter, you fhould think proper to bring it into the houfe of Lords, or into the court of King's Bench*.—But, my Lord, you dare not do either.

JUNIUS.

* A short time before the publication of the two preceding letters, the Duke of Grafton had commenced a profecution againft Mr. Samuel Vaughan, for attempting to corrupt him by an offer of 5000l. for a patent place in Jamaica. When the rule to fhew caufe, why an information fhould not be exhibited againft Vaughan, was argued in the King's Bench, Nov. 27th, 1769, by the opinion of the four judges, the rule was made abfolute. The following accurate extract from Lord Mansfield's
fpeech

speech on the occasion, deserves attention. "A practice of the kind complained of here is certainly dishonourable and scandalous.—If a man, standing under the relation of an officer under the King, or of a
person in whom the King puts confidence, or of a
minister, takes money for the use of that confidence
the King puts in him, he basely betrays the King,—
he basely betrays his trust.—If the King sold the
office, it would be acting contrary to the trust the
constitution hath reposed in him. The constitution
does not intend the crown should sell those offices, to
raise a revenue out of them.—Is it possible to hesitate, whether this would not be criminal in the Duke
of Grafton;—contrary to his duty as a privy counsellor;—contrary to his duty as a minister;—contrary
to his duty as a subject?—His advice should be free
according to his judgement;—It is the duty of his
office;—he has sworn to it."—Notwithstanding this,
the Duke is positively said by Junius to have sold a patent place to Mr. Hine for 3500l. and yet was Lord
Privy Seal when this letter was written. If the house
of commons had impeached the Duke as they ought to
have done, Lord Mansfield would have been in a most
ridiculous situation. On Junius's discovery and publication of the Duke's conduct, the prosecution against
Vaughan was dropped, on purpose it is said to save
both the Judge and the Duke.

End of Volume I.

www.ingramcontent.com/pod-product-compliance
Lightning Source LLC
Chambersburg PA
CBHW031946230426
43672CB00010B/2068